The Modern School Library

Its Administration as a Materials Center

By

Helen E. Saunders

The Scarecrow Press, Inc.
Metuchen, N. J. 1968

L. C. Card No. 68-12623

Preface

This book is designed as a text for the basic course in library administration required for students preparing for school librarianship, particularly those interested in working in secondary schools. It is thought of either as an introduction to the courses concerned with selection, organization and use in the school librarianship curriculum, or as the final course in this program.

Although there are chapters on selecting and organizing materials as well as on housing the library, the emphasis is on library service. The goal of the school library administrator is effective utilization of the materials and services by every student and teacher in the school; consequently, all other activities of the library lead to this objective.

Few courses can be taught exclusively with one text, so the selected readings and audiovisual materials listed for further study at the ends of chapters are an important part of the book.

The philosophy that all learning materials in a school be under one administration is basic to this book. Whether or not these materials are located in one place is a secondary matter; but the fragmentation which takes place when textbooks are administered by one person, audiovisual aids by another, and printed materials by the librarian discourages the best use of all aids to learning. That these materials and guidance in their use is best administered under the direction of the librarian seems natural to the author.

The author would have been unable to write this book without the fine collection in the field of librarianship located in the Zimmerman Library of the University of New Mexico. The professional library in the Central Office of the Albuquerque Public Schools and at Valley High School were also of much assistance, particularly the periodical collections.

The inspiration and encouragement of Paul Saunders, the author's husband, made the writing of this book a reality. It would have been largely a passing thought, were it not for his sincere interest as well as his knowledgeability and help in the actual writing.

Helen E. Saunders

Albuquerque, New Mexico
June 1967

Table of Contents

Chapter I

What is a Good School Library Program?

Libraries have been in existence for thousands of years. Egyptian records show that libraries existed there as long as five thousand years ago. Archaeologists have found evidence of collections of clay tablets in the temple libraries of Babylonia around 650 B. C. The papyrus rolls of the famous Alexandrian libraries numbered nearly seven thousand. With the development of parchment came the establishment of great church and monastery libraries during the first few centuries of the Christian Era. Although the librarians and book collectors considered printed books inferior to the hand-written parchment manuscripts, by the year 1500 these printed books made up the major collection of libraries. Along with the ability of large numbers of people to read and the American concept of public education for everyone, came the growth of the public library where printed materials were available to all. During the latter half of the nineteenth century, the importance of public libraries was recognized when several states allowed for tax supported libraries. As technology produced films and recordings, some adventurous librarians experimented with adding them to their collections; but by far the majority of libraries were largely depositories for books and other printed materials until around 1950.

However, as long ago as 1947, California recognized the need for facilities and staffs for providing book and audiovisual services. At that time the California legislature established the County School Service Fund which resulted in setting up county-level instructional materials centers under the direction of certified librarians. This recognition of the materials center concept led the way for the establishment of similar centers at the district and individual school level.

Recognition of the Materials Center Concept

The concept of the central school library as a place where all kinds of learning materials are found was recognized in 1956 when an official statement formalizing the concept was issued by the American Association of School Librarians. Furthermore, the executive boards of the American Association of School Librarians and the Association of College and Research Libraries--both divisions of the American Library Association--and the Department of Audiovisual Instruction of the National Education Association approved a statement in 1958 emphasizing the same approach to library materials. Finally, in 1960 the American Association of School Librarians, in cooperation with nineteen other groups, produced the _Standards for School Library Programs,_ recognizing the incorporation of all learning materials in the library. These _Standards_ also incorporated quantitative criteria for audiovisual as well as printed materials.[1] Standards for non-print media were adopted in 1965 by the Department of Audiovisual Instruction of the National Education Association and the Association of Chief State School Audiovisual Officers in a detailed statement entitled "Quantitative Standards for Audiovisual Personnel, Equipment and Materials."

In 1966 a revision of the AASL _Standards_ was announced, under the chairmanship of Dr. Frances Henne of Columbia University's Graduate Library School. Following recent developments in teaching methods, curriculum and school organization, the new standards will "include special programs for preschool, underprivileged and exceptional youth; recognize cooperative developments in regional planning; and incorporate the impact of Federal and state legislation on libraries and education."[2]

In reference to the five regional accrediting associations which set standards for colleges and secondary schools, various statements about school libraries are included.[3] In the accreditation process, a school's total program is evaluated, including the library; however, a school may receive accreditation even though it does not meet the library requirements, provided it shows evidence of library improvement.

State Departments of Education

The functions of state departments of education are described in a policy statement concerning school library services published in 1961 by the Council of Chief State School Officers. It stands firmly in favor of the centralized library as against the individual classroom library, and favors the school library as a center for all instructional materials, under the direction of professionally trained personnel. The majority of the State departments of education have developed a wide variety of standards, most of which are a part of the general school standards for the state rather than separate school library standards.[4] Between the publication of the original Standards for School Library Programs in 1960 and 1962, twenty-three states revised their existing standards or wrote new ones.[5] At this writing, other states are making studies and holding meetings toward plans for improving their standards for school libraries.

Finally the role of state librarians' associations in influencing standards at both the state and local levels should not be underestimated. Although standards set up by them usually do not have offficial status, they are often used by the local schools. The school librarians' associations of California, Michigan, and New York have been particularly strong in this field.

Most of the national, regional, state, and professional associations agree on the broad base for this new concept of the materials center. All learning materials in a school should be incorporated into one centrally located area which provides for their acquisition, processing, storage, repair and use. However, as the enrollment of a high school increases or when a school installs flexible scheduling with large group instruction, small group discussion and considerable individual study as advocated by J. Lloyd Trump[6], decentralization by broad subject area is recommended.

Materials Center Defined

Regardless of whether the collection is in one location or is decentralized, all kinds of media are incorporated: books, magazines, pamphlets, newspapers, pictures, maps, college catalogs, films, filmstrips, disc and tape recordings, slides and realia. With the broadening of the collection to include non-print material has come a new name for the library: the instructional materials center. Other names used are: the educational media center, learning materials center, educational resource center and a confusing variation of these terms. New school plants are apt to use a new name; others continue to use the old term, library, despite the incorporation of all kinds of new media. We shall use the old name, library, in this book.

Evaluation of the Library Program

How does a school find out if its library reflects the standards set up by the various groups above? In the first place, an accurate picture of the existing library conditions must be drawn. In secondary schools, the use of the form "Instructional Materials Service," from Evaluative Criteria published in 1960 by the National Study of Secondary School Evaluation, is recommended. Here are outlined criteria for evaluating the instructional materials staff, organization and management, accessibility of instructional materials services, the materials themselves, physical facilities, and special characteristics of instructional materials services.[7] With a complete picture of the existing facility in mind, a comparison must be made with the national, regional and state standards. If the library falls far below in some or all areas, the facts must be brought to the attention of the community, the board of education, the superintendent of schools, the local administrators, faculty and students. It must be recognized that the chief resource group upon which the community will rely is inevitably the local school library staff.

The impetus in raising standards of local school libraries has gained considerably in the 1960's from a number of pilot experiments sponsored by various organizations.

Projects to Update School Libraries

Two projects sponsored by the American Library Association gave great momentum to school library development. Financed by a grant of $100,000 from the Council on Library Resources, Inc., the School Library Development Project over a period of eighteen months had as its chief purpose the encouragement of each state to adopt sound, up-to-date standards for school libraries. In order to accomplish this purpose, the Project promoted an understanding of the 1960 Standards; showed how a team approach by lay groups, educators and librarians could be used; developed techniques and printed and audiovisual materials to be used in raising the standards of the local library. All states were invited to submit proposals for self-implementation of the Standards, and twenty-one grants were made, totaling $12,000 to assist their work. These projects included conferences and workshops with groups of educators and citizens, surveys and evaluations of existing local programs. In addition to providing consultant service under the leadership of the Project Director, Mrs. Frances Kennon Johnson, numerous printed materials were made available, including: "Ten Steps in School Library Development," "Achieving Quality in School Library Programs," "Individual School Guide for Planning School Library Development," "Planning for Elementary Libraries for a School System," "Plan for Improving Service in a High School." Although some of these are now out of print, others are still available and of practical use in making plans to improve school library service today.

The other ALA project, financed by a 1963 grant of $1,130,000 from the Knapp Foundation, provides for a five-year demonstration of the optimum educational value of school library services. The first two years of the Knapp School Libraries Project with emphasis on the elementary school library saw the selection of five schools from over one hundred applicants. Each one had previously made some effort toward library improvement. Each school used the funds as needed in its own unique situation. After the library program thus strengthened was put into action, the Project provided opportunities for groups of people to visit the school. A faculty member from a nearby teacher education institution was employed half-time to serve as the Field Worker to coordinate these visits. Each visiting team was able to apply for reimbursement of its expenses incurred in transportation, lodging and meals for the one-day visit to a Project school in its general geographical area. The school was to make detailed plans for the visitors, provide factual information for each team member before the group arrived, and on the day of the visit see to it that the library itself could be thoroughly examined, the staff conferred with and the library watched in action. The principal and teachers were to be made available for conferences. Classes were to be visited and children informally interviewed.

One of the elementary schools receiving the benefits of the Knapp School Libraries Project was the Casis School in Austin, Texas. The Austin school system has supported elementary school libraries and librarians since 1953. Casis has served as a laboratory school of the University of Texas since it opened in 1951, with a well organized and functioning library program. Nevertheless, it had developed a strong library program over the years largely as a "bootstrap" operation with the help of teachers and parents and the leadership of an outstanding librarian. For service to 750 pupils in kindergarten through the sixth grade and a teaching staff of thirty-nine, the Knapp Project made available the services of three full-time librarians and one full-time clerk, where previously there was one librarian and one assistant librarian. The materials collection was increased and expanded, particularly in non-print media, so that by the fall of 1965 there were 12,000 books in the collection and over 1500 tapes, filmstrips and other audiovisual aids. The quarters themselves were increased to 3800 square feet, including a study center, classroom, informal story-telling and reading area, and a listening center.

When a group from Albuquerque, New Mexico, visited Casis School in February, 1966, the members were able to confer with Dr. M. G. Bowden, the school's principal, with Dr. Alma Freeland, the Field Worker from the University of Texas, classroom teachers and the library staff. At one time during the day, the members saw three group activities going on at the same time in the library. Dr. Alice Brooks McGuire, the librarian, was working in the listening center in the final phase of a special unit for a small group of able sixth graders. One of the assistant librarians was talking about books to an entire class which was visiting the library. A parent volunteer was telling stories to another group. At the same time, individual children were coming into the library, going about their business, with the other assistant librarian being available for help as needed. The children needed no help in checking out their materials as the self-help system was used. Meanwhile, the library secretary was working with new materials in order to make them quickly available for use. Since most of the children had ten library orientation lessons during the first semester, it was obvious from the way they acted that they were very much at home in the library. In addition, they and their teachers had come to the library for briefing, as a new unit was introduced. In materials, quarters and personnel, the Casis School now met the AASL Standards quantitatively; as a result, the quality of the library program reflected more nearly the character and quality of education at Casis.

In 1965 the Knapp School Libraries Project selected three secondary schools to be assisted in the same way that the elementary ones were. After the Knapp demonstration schools have been in existence for two years, there is a commitment on the part of the local school authorities to maintain financial assistance at the same level as provided by the Knapp funds.

Project Discovery

An experiment known as Project Discovery, now being conducted with large numbers of audiovisual aids, is another study of interest to schools wanting to improve their library programs. During a three-year period, Encyclopaedia Britannica Films is providing its entire film and filmstrip collection for four school districts located in California, Ohio, Texas and Washington, D. C. Each of the school districts meets AASL Standards. In each classroom, Bell and Howell has placed a filmstrip projector, a 16mm film projector and a projection table and screen. The schools are being studied by the Educational Research Bureau of Ohio State University to see what effect the availability of these materials will have on teaching methods, on student achievement, and on the general attitude toward non-print media. In Terrell, Texas, an entire school year was spent in weekly workshops for the teachers prior to the beginning of Project Discovery, so that the films and filmstrips could be previewed and when and how to use them discussed. As the Terrell project completed its first year of operation in June, 1965, it was discovered that there was favorable reaction on all grade levels. In the primary grades vocabulary and reading readiness were increased, while in the senior high school the students' interests were held to such an extent that the drop-out rate was reduced. As audiovisual material in quantity is available both for home and school use, it will be interesting to watch for the results which available research on Project Discovery will reveal at its completion in 1967.

School-Public Library Relations

Even though library services for students both in relation to curriculum requirements and personal interests should be available in every local school, many children and young people use their community's public library in addition to their school library. The necessity for communication and understanding between the school and the public library is therefore very important. One effort in this direction is the statement adopted in 1961 by the Council of Chief State School Officers:

> The school library serves the school, and the public library serves the community. Teachers and pupils are members of both the school and the community.
>
> Public library service--including service from state, regional, county, and community libraries--may supplement but never supplant the school library. Service which replaces the school library impedes the development of school libraries to the detriment of service to teachers and pupils and tends to separate library materials from instructional programs.
>
> The school has the primary responsibility for instruction and guidance of children and youth in the community in the use of libraries. The program of library instruction, directed by the school librarians, has the broad purposes of teaching library skills adaptable to all types of libraries and for encouraging pupils to use libraries for continuing self-education. School librarians, teachers, and public librarians should cooperate in planning instructional programs in the use of libraries for educational and recreational purposes.
>
> Cooperative planning in the selection and utilization of materials for children and young people is the responsibility of school administrators, teachers, school librarians, public librarians, and other community leaders concerned with youth.[8]

This statement is to be implemented in various ways. In some communities, school and public librarians work together on selection by evaluating new materials and sharing their opinions in monthly discussions. Expensive reference titles primarily of an adult nature are purchased by the public library but are readily available for the selected students who can make use of them. More popular reference titles are found in quantity in the school library, thus releasing these volumes for adult use in the public library. The school sees to it that multiple copies of certain titles on teachers' required reading lists are purchased. This shared evaluation and purchase of new materials can also be worked out on a multi-county or statewide basis.

The extent to which public libraries and publicly supported colleges are willing and able to serve high school students varies considerably. According to Richard C. Quick's report on the survey made by the American Library Association's College Libraries Section, "The community group that appears closest to being genuinely unwelcome in the American college and university library is the high school student segment. . ."[9] With the very rapid growth in numbers of students enrolled in colleges and universities, many of these libraries are having a difficult time serving their own faculty and students. Even when they are willing to do so, the problem of adequate financial support seems to plague the public library also, making it difficult to meet the demands for materials and guidance as requested by the student. One suggestion has been made that the school library meet the students' curriculum related needs and the public library their recreational needs.

At the national level some of the recent federal grants require that school libraries work with other libraries. The amendment to Title III of the Library Services and Construction Act provides for the coordination of the resources of school, public, academic and special libraries for improved services which supplement those now given to the special users of each kind of library. Under Title II of the Elementary and Secondary Education Act as extended in 1966, programs must be coordinated at both the local and state levels with the Library Services and Construction Act.

When school library services are inadequate as far as number and kind of materials, hours of opening, floor space, etc., there is no doubt that a great burden is placed on the public library and on any college or special libraries in the community. When teachers have the habit of telling the school library staff about their library-related assignments, the librarians in turn have the responsibility of notifying the other libraries in the community. This may mean simply a few phone calls; but it is a good idea to send a monthly summary in writing to the public library, giving specific information as to type of assignment, requirements, date assignment is due and teacher's name. When school and public librarians periodically meet together, attempts can be made to solve such problems as abuse of materials, unreasonable demands, seating space for adults using the public library after school hours, and the increasing cost of library materials.

What are the possibilities of inter-school library cooperation within a community? Librarians new to a school system should feel free to ask others for information or advice. It is relatively easy to borrow materials. Librarians in elementary and junior high schools of a geographical area of the city must meet frequently with the library staff of the senior high school in the same area to talk together about the unique needs of their students, to work out a developmental program of library instruction, and to see how unnecessary duplication of effort can be eliminated.

As the population continues to move into large urban centers, the need for inter-library cooperation will increase. The major key to this cooperation is communication. Much can be accomplished when librarians help each other but it cannot be done without constant effort toward communication and understanding. Reading about what other school libraries do, evaluating and measuring our service against standards, attending meetings where we talk with other librarians and receive inspiration from national leaders, all provide knowledge that can be adapted to the local situation.

The responsibilities of the school library administrator are multitudinous. He must see to it that all kinds of materials are carefully selected, ordered, organized and made available for use. However, these responsibilities are the means to a greater responsibility: the best possible use of the library's materials and services to meet the goals of the local school.

Notes

1. American Association of School Librarians, Standards for School Library Programs. Chicago: American Library Association, 1960, pp. 24-25.

2. "The New Standards" (Editorial) Library Journal, XCI (September 15, 1966), 4154.

3. Richard L. Darling, Survey of School Library Standards, U. S. Office of Education Circular No. 740, Washington, D. C.: U. S. Government Printing Office, 1964, pp. 30-34.

4. Ibid., 175.

5. Ibid., 4.

6. J. Lloyd Trump and Dorsey Baynham, Focus on Change: Guide to Better Schools. Chicago: Rand McNally and Co., 1961.

7. National Study of Secondary School Evaluation, Evaluative Criteria, Washington, D. C., 1960.

8. Responsibilities of State Departments of Education for Library Services, Washington, D. C.: Council of Chief State School Officers, 1961, pp. 14-15.

9. "A Many-Splintered Thing" (Editorial) Library Journal, XCI (August, 1966), 3663.

Selected Audiovisual Materials

The Modern School Library

* Are Libraries Doing Enough? 16mm film; sound, black and white, 30 min. 1962. Maryland Library Association.

  A discussion of what libraries are doing and how they can improve their services. Filmed as a part of Maryland's observance of National Library Week.

* The Elementary School Library. Filmstrip; 78 frames, script and record, color. 1962. Atlantis Productions, Inc., 894 Sheffield Pl., Thousand Oaks, Calif. 91360

  The photographs and commentary show children using well-equipped library facilities in four California school districts. Produced jointly by the School Library Association of California and the California State Department of Education.

* School Libraries. Filmstrip; 30 frames, silent with script, black and white. 1964. UNESCO, Place de Fontenoy, Paris 7ᵉ, France.

  Explains the essential functions of the school library and shows the important contribution it can make to the educational growth of the child.

Wanted and Needed - A School Library. 16mm film; sound, color, 30 min. 1960. Produced by Orange County, Florida, Council of School Librarians and the Orange County Materials Center, 312 N. Rosalind St., Orlando, Florida. 32801

  Shows the growth of centralized libraries for junior and senior high schools and emphasizes the need for the same kind of libraries for elementary schools.

Standards

* The Fenton Story: How a Community Developed Good School Libraries. Filmstrip; 52 frames, silent with captions, color. 1962. Produced by the Michigan Association of School Librarians. Obtainable from Kenneth Vance, Bureau of School Library Services, University of Michigan, Ann Arbor, Michigan. 48106

  Shows how a small Michigan town improved its school libaries with the aid of AASL's Standards for School Library Programs.

* School Library Standards. Tape. 3 3/4 speed, 25 min.

  Address given by Frances Henne at ALA Conference, Washington, D.C., 1959.

Gives philosophy, background and highlights of the 1960 school library standards.

School Library Development Project

* Kennon, Mary Frances, Speech. Tape. 3 3/4 speed, 30 min.

A talk on school library standards delivered at the University of San Francisco, May 31, 1962.

* Next Steps in School Library Development. Tape. 3 3/4 speed, 30 min.

A talk by Frances Henne at the School Library Development Project Conference, Spring, 1961.

* School Library Development Project. 3 sets of slides and tapes. 35 mm color slides with narrative script. Titles: Good Elementary School Library, Good High School Library, We Serve our School.

Sponsored by the American Association of School Librarians, the sets can be used as program material for meetings of librarians, teachers, administrators and lay groups interested in school libraries. The sets aim to interpret the functions of the school library and to initiate discussion of school library service.

Knapp School Libraries Project

* ...And Something More. 16 mm film. sound, color, 28 min. 1965. Knapp School Libraries Project. Cleared for TV. Produced by Guggenheim Productions, Inc. Prints are available on free loan from Modern Talking Picture Service, Inc., Concourse Shop No. 7, 10 Rockefeller Plaza, New York, N. Y., 10020, and its numerous offices throughout the country.

Using the Sedgefield Elementary School of Charlotte, North Carolina, the film demonstrates the impact of good school library service on teachers and students.

* Living School Libraries. Filmstrip; 41 frames, sound, color. 1965. American Library Association.

A progress report of school library development under the Knapp School Libraries Project. Pictures of the many aspects of library programs in the elementary school libraries of Phase I and Phase II.

* Three for Tomorrow. Filmstrip; 95 frames, color with recorded script. 1966. American Library Association.

Visit to the three secondary schools participating in Phase

III of the Knapp School Libraries Project: Roosevelt High School, Portland, Oregon; Farrer Junior High School, Provo, Utah; Oak Park and River Forest High School, Oak Park, Illinois.

Project Discovery and School Library Awards Program

* The Challenge; Encyclopaedia Britannica School Library Awards. Filmstrip. 67 frames, color with recorded script. 1966. Encyclopaedia Britannica Educational Corporation.

Describes highlights of the School Library Awards Program.

Project Discovery I. 16mm film; color, 28 min. 1966. Encyclopaedia Britannica Films.

Shows the Project in action at Mercer School.

* Available on loan for round-trip shipping costs from Headquarters Library, American Library Association, 50 East Huron St., Chicago, Illinois. 60611. In the case of films, there is also a three-dollar fee.

Selected Readings

The Modern School Library

Asheim, Lester. "Reading and the Newer Media," ALA Bulletin, LV (February, 1961), 148-152.

Objective study of contrasting values of various media.

Butler, Kenneth W. "A Modest Proposal for a Contemporary School Library," Education, LXXXVI (March, 1966), 417-420.

Need for all learning materials to be organized into one service. Comments on finances, materials, physical facilities, and staff for such a center.

Chicago. University. Graduate Library School. 24th Conference. New Definitions in School Library Service. Edited by Sara I. Fenwick. Chicago: University of Chicago Press, 1960.

Ellsworth, Ralph E. The School Library. Washington, D.C.: The Center for Applied Research in Education, Inc., 1965.

Gaver, Mary V. Effectiveness of Centralized Library Service in Elementary Schools. 2nd edition. New Brunswick, New Jersey: Rutgers University Press, 1963.

________ Patterns of Development in Elementary School Libraries Today. 2nd edition. Chicago: Encyclopaedia Britannica, Inc., 1965.

Hartz, F. R. and R. T. Samuelson. "Origin, Development and Present State of the Secondary School Library as a Materials Center," Peabody Journal of Education, XLIII (July, 1965), 33-39.

Illinois. University. Graduate School of Library Science. The School Library Materials Center: Its Resources and Their Utilization... Edited by Alice Lohrer. Distributed by The Illini Union Bookstore, Champaign, Illinois. 61801. 1963.

Lowrie, Jean E. Elementary School Libraries. New York: The Scarecrow Press, Inc., 1961.

National Association of Secondary School Principals. Libraries in Secondary Schools... Washington, D. C.: National Education Association, 1966.

National Study of Secondary School Evaluation. Evaluative Criteria. 1960 edition. Washington, D. C.: The Study, pp. 257-272.

Pacific Northwest Library Association. Elementary and Secondary School Libraries of the Pacific Northwest. (Library Development Project Reports Vol. II) Seattle: University of Washington Press, 1960.

Research Reports. National Defense Education Act Title VII, New Educational Media. 8th special edition. Washington, D. C.: U. S. Government Printing Office, 1965.

Abstracts of 37 federally funded projects on utilization of audiovisual media for educational purposes.

State Department of Education Leadership in Developing the Use of New Educational Media. Washington, D. C.: Council of Chief State School Officers, 1964.

Statement of AASL's Philosophy of School Libraries as a Materials Center. Chicago: American Association of School Librarians, 1956. (mimeographed)

Trinkner, Charles L. Better Libraries Make Better Schools. Hamden, Connecticut: Shoe String Press, Inc., 1962.

Standards

Ahlers, Eleanor E. "Story of a Survey," School Libraries, XIII (May, 1964), pp. 19-29.

Survey of school library and audiovisual programs in the state of Washington.

American Association of School Librarians. Standards for School Library Programs. Chicago: American Library Association, 1960.

Criteria Relating to Educational Media Programs in School Systems. Washington, D. C.: Department of Audiovisual Instruction, National Education Association, 1966.

Darling, Richard L. Survey of School Library Standards. U. S. Dept. of Health, Education and Welfare. Distributed by U. S. Government Printing Office, 1964.

Fulton, W. R. Evaluative Checklist: An Instrument for Self-evaluating an Educational Media Program in School Systems. Washington, D. C.: Department of Audiovisual Instruction, National Education Association, 1966.

Mahar, Mary H. "Inventory of Library Needs - School Libraries." In United States. Education Office. Library Services Branch. National Inventory of Library Needs. Chicago: American Library Association, 1965, pp. 23-37.

Quantitative Standards for Audiovisual Personnel, Equipment and Materials. Washington, D. C.: Department of Audiovisual Instruction, National Education Association, 1966. (mimeographed)

Responsibilities of State Departments of Education for School Library Services. Washington, D. C.: Council of Chief State School Officers, 1961.

Sherman, Mendel and Gene Faris. "Standards and Evaluative Instruments for Audiovisual Programs," School Libraries XV (May, 1966), 25-29.

School Library Development Project

Johnson, Frances Kennon. Planning School Library Development. Chicago: American Association of School Librarians, 1962.

__________. "Principles of School Library Development," School Libraries, XII (October, 1962), 23-26.

__________. "SLDP - a Progress Report," School Libraries, XI (October, 1961), 25-27.

School Library Development Project publications (mimeographed or printed) as follows:

"Achieving Quality in School Library Programs: The Leadership Role of School Librarians"

"Individual School Guide for Planning School Library Development"

"Man the Pumps! A Proposed Plan for Elementary School Library Development"

"Plan for Improving Library Service in a High School"

"Planning for Elementary Libraries for a School System"

Single copies of the foregoing are available free from the American Association of School Librarians.

Knapp School Libraries Project

Crawford, L. E. "Knapp School Libraries Project: Functional Staffing for a High School Library," School Libraries, XV (March, 1966), 27-33.

Goodwin, G. J. "Knapp Project at Allisonville, Indiana," School Libraries, XV (May, 1966), 38-39.

McGuire, A. B. "New Wing at Casis," [Austin, Texas] Library Journal, XC (December15, 1965), 5460-5462.

Sullivan, Peggy. Impact: The School Library and the Instructional Program. Chicago: American Library Association, 1967.

__________. "Knapp High Schools and the ALA Standards," Library Journal, XCI (May 15, 1966), 2609-2611.

Project Discovery

Brill, James A. "What is Project Discovery?" Scholastic Teacher, LXXXIX (October 7, 1966), Sup. 8

"Discovery: A Study in Audiovisual Saturation," Library Journal, XCII (February 15, 1967), 849-852.

Muller, R. D. "Project Discovery: Experiment in Learning," California School Libraries, XXXVI (March, 1965), 38-40.

School and Public Library Relations

Lacy, Dan. "Impact of Universal Education; remarks, June 1965," Library Journal, XCI (September 1, 1966), 3866-3870.

Lindauer, D. C. "Sample Projects: Title III, ESEA: Nassau School-Public Library Project," Library Journal, XCI (February 15, 1966), 1024-1028.

McJenkin, Virginia, editor. Service to Students; Joint Responsibility of School and Public Libraries. Chicago: American Association of School Librarians.

A reprint of articles appearing in the ALA Bulletin, June, 1965-January, 1966.

Martin, Lowell, Students and the Pratt Library: Challenge and

Opportunity. Baltimore, Maryland: Enoch Pratt Free Library, 1963.

Van Every, Joan, "School-Public Library Cooperation in Santa Monica," California School Libraries, XXXIV (May, 1963), 16-19.

One of seven articles on "How Public Libraries Serve the Schools."

"Young Adult Services: A Symposium," Top of the News, XXII (June, 1966), 349-363.

Five articles on current status of services to young adults in public libraries. Also available as a reprint from Young Adult Services Division, ALA.

Chapter II

The Librarian as Counselor and Teacher

The chief responsibility of secondary school librarians is to serve as teachers in the broadest concept. For this reason, they need to know the characteristics of growth from childhood to adulthood, particularly development during adolescence. When they really understand adolescent growth, they will not be easily shocked or amazed at teenagers' reactions to the library. It is easy to stereotype adolescents but the librarian must realize that all are individuals. Flexibility is demanded of the librarian who accepts the fact that one student at a table may still be a child, while at the other end there may be one whose maturity is very noticeable. An awareness that adolescence is a time of change must be realized and that many teenagers will have different reactions and different needs next month or next year.

Acceptance by librarians of young people from all kinds of backgrounds is necessary. When the librarian does not understand or will not accept the student from a low socio-economic background, he is shirking his responsibility of service to meet the needs of each student in his school. The same holds true for the librarian who thinks that because a teenager has the advantage of well-educated parents, many books in his home, and an annual trip abroad, there is nothing the school library can provide for him. Librarians must take each student where he is in order to give individual guidance.

Materials for Teenagers

When librarians accept teenagers as individuals, they provide materials and services to meet each need. As publishers and producers became aware of the teenager as a special library client, they have made available materials especially suited to his needs, such as the books by James Kjelgaard, John Tunis, Anne Emory and Mary Stolz, all of which are books of real merit, written for the adolescent. Some materials, however, have been produced by "hack" writers for publishers who were in a hurry to get on this particular "bandwagon," resulting occasionally in "intellectual pablum." There is a great need for good materials written and produced in all subject areas particularly for adolescent consumption.

Need for a Variety of Media

When libraries contain various kinds of media, they are more likely to meet the needs of the student as far as both his personal interests and his curriculum related requirements are concerned. The learning process comes about through the use of all the senses--through listening, hearing, seeing, smelling and feeling. In the difficult process of learning, the student must be an active participant. Since learning is an individual and private thing, what may aid the process with one student may not with another. The appeal of one medium over another varies from student to student. Hence, a variety of media easily available in the school library is a necessity. Books and other printed materials are basic to any library collection. The printed word is the major means through which formal education is acquired. Reading is used constantly by young and old in every day life. Books are published in vast numbers and are readily available for purchase. Books can be carried easily with a person wherever he goes, and by the simple turning of a page the reader is able to read and re-read for any length of time. All other materials are used to enrich, to supplement, and to make more meaningful the learning process.

Programmed learning, whether in book or other form, has the advantage of step-by-step, independent study, easily used by an individual at his own rate of speed. Programmed instruction is being tried in ungraded programs, in homework, in the laboratory and for self-correction.

Pictures have the flexibility of ease of handling, passing around in a group and posting on a board for independent study.

The popular appeal of a good film as a means of arousing an emotional response in the viewer, so that he becomes an active learner, cannot be denied. The filmstrip and the slide also appeal to the sight. Since each frame can be examined for an indefinite length of time and one can go back to re-examine any frame, they are very practical.

Recordings, both disc and tape, may attract the attention of the student when no other medium can. The tremendous number of recordings purchased by young people witnesses to their value.

Multi-media kits containing--in the field of archaeology, for example--books, films, pictures, tapes, and objects such as stones, wood and pottery, are among the newest materials in the library.

It is not a matter of which shall the library contain--printed or non-print materials; nor is it a matter of one material being better than another *per se*. One material is superior to another in terms of a specific need or a particular teaching situation. Can a particular need be met best by a film? Does hearing a tape recording lead the listener to consult other media to reinforce or to extend an idea? The librarian's task is to guide the student to the material best suited for his needs.

Development of Interest in Reading

How best to go about guiding the young adult is a problem which librarians and teachers frequently discuss. Many high schools have as one of their goals the encouragement of reading as a lifetime habit. Yet the way they go about it may lead the students to hate reading. In a speech given by G. Robert Carlsen at the American Library Association Conference in 1964, a thoughtful presentation of adolescent reading was revealed.[1] Dr. Carlsen, in reporting on the reading interests of young adults aged sixteen to twenty, pointed out that studies have revealed the failure of traditional reading programs to develop enthusiasm for reading. Far too many teachers actually encourage the adolescents' dislike for reading through the use of required book lists; detailed, lengthy reading and analysis of works for which the students are not ready; and memorization of selections they do not understand. Required book lists in themselves are not bad. What is bad about them is that often they are too limited in some way. They may consist only of adult books, too difficult for many students to read. Perhaps the list is too short and hence there is little choice. In the compilation of some lists, the reading ability of the students to whom they are given has not been considered. When class study requires detailed analysis of a book the student may come to think of reading as an exercise in word study. According to Dr. Carlsen, a study of the general pattern of growth in reading tastes shows what the first reading satisfaction of young people is in the typical adolescent book. Then he grows toward the popular adult book, followed by the reading of serious contemporary literature. These latter stages are where most young adults are reading, said Dr. Carlsen. Finally, the reader becomes interested in the classics as the final step in his maturity, but too often this stage is forced upon the reader far before he is mature enough to grasp it. Dr. Carlsen said that young adults are reading largely adult books on the basis of their content in human experience. The kinds of books they read deal with individuals who are looking for a sense of direction; with social problems; with the unusual; and with the transition from adolescence into early adult life. Dr. Carlsen's plea for letting the young adult read what he is ready for, rather than forcing him into literature beyond his ability to comprehend or appreciate, is a point to be seriously considered in reading guidance.

A conference of the Committee on Reading Development of the National Book Committee, held in 1954 for the purpose of discussing the role of secondary education in developing or encouraging lasting habits of book-reading, reported some interesting findings which are as applicable today as they were when the report was published. The report of the Committee was published by the R. R. Bowker Company under the title "The Development of Lifetime Reading Habits," written by Jean D. Grambs. Unfortunately, it is no longer in print. It reported that the influence of three factors is felt in the role of reading and the schools: the competence and interest of teachers in the developing of reading habits, the availability of books for purchase, and the kind and quality of library or other book service. In considering the first factor, the Report suggests that there are many ways in which interest in reading can be killed as well as fostered, such as spending a long time studying one book. When this is done, the value of a work of literature may be lost and the interest and enjoyment of reading may be discouraged.

Young people need to have experiences of reading many books--many of which may be superficial--and of talking about what they read. Thus critical judgement can be developed. The reading habit must be established through the reading of a wide range of books, and then standards of taste will develop. As more and more inexpensive books are made available for purchase by young people and as school library development expands, there will be a greater chance for the development of reading as a lifetime habit.

Any high school is apt to have students whose special needs must be met through guidance in the library as well as in the classroom and elsewhere in the school. In a school system where there is a strong library program beginning in the first grade, the demand for guidance in the secondary school may be largely curriculum related. But high school librarians receive many questions of a personal or social nature, unique to the adolescent, which lead to informal guidance in these areas. Information on dress, careers, and how to run for an office are among the requests often received. However, one of the major goals of the elementary school library is to inculcate a love of reading and a realization that the answer to anything about which one is curious can be found in a library. If the elementary library is successful, the young person will already have the "library habit." But in his needs in relation to the subjects he is studying, he will require considerable help. First of all, students with special needs must be identified: the culturally disadvantaged, the exceptional, the reluctant reader, the gifted, the non-achiever. Librarians need to look over the students' cumulative records usually available in the counselor's or principal's office, which contain anecdotal records, intelligence quotients, reading scores, and other information leading to greater knowledge of each student's abilities and interests. For the non-achiever, inability to read well is apt to be a basic reason for lack of achievement; therefore, the library must contain books and magazines of high interest to the teenager but with a low vocabulary. The magazine _Scope_, designed for junior and senior high school students who are several years behind in reading ability, is an example of this kind of printed material.[2] Finding out the interests of the non-achiever--and therefore, the potential dropout--is fundamental to helping him. Then finding books, films, pictures, etc., on his interests is one big step in helping him to achieve success. Sometimes newspapers, pamphlets, and other materials of a practical how-to-do-it nature appeal to this teenager. The non-achiever may have the ability to learn, but he has not done so through lack of motivation.

As efforts have been made to meet the needs for improved health, housing and employment for many of our citizens, so also is the special need of the child from limited cultural background met by the school library program. Simple recognition by schools of the great contribution which can be made in this area alone has caused more money to be spent on libraries in recent years. In the thickly populated state of Pennsylvania, for example, where formerly only 28.4 percent of the high school graduates went to college, library development is described by John Rowell, formerly Director of School Libraries, Pennsylvania State Department of Public Instruction.[3] Provision has been made there for school library resources for all children regardless of their economic or cultural circumstances. During the first year of its expanded library program, one Pennsylvania county had a library budget of $12.31 per pupil.

Meeting the Needs of the Non-achiever

Even getting the non-achievers and the culturally disadvantaged to come into the library is a problem. Speaking to them in the halls, in the cafeteria, and commenting on their success in athletics, for example, can show that the librarian is really interested in them. They may then realize that they, too, are welcome in the library. When there are appealing displays and attractive materials of all kinds, the library turns out to be something other than a formidable place associated by the non-achiever with difficult classroom activities. Then it is up to the library staff to see to it that these students get some kind of satisfying experience the very first time they enter the library. A great deal of individual guidance is needed if their visit is to result in making the library a place where they like to come, and where they can achieve some kind of success. Such experiences may result in their staying in school until graduation.

Meeting the Needs of the Gifted

When working with gifted students, librarians quickly find that they can usually be expected to excel in reading, and they may do a great deal more reading than average students. Getting the omnivorous reader to react thoughtfully and intelligently to what is read is a real challenge. If the library contains books with thought-provoking ideas, then teachers and librarians must provide opportunities for students to interpret what they read. Relating what is read to other experiences such as movies, television programs and trips is good. Opportunities must be provided for independent reading during the school day. Just because a student is able to read adult materials, it may not follow that he has the intellectual and emotional maturity to understand them, particularly in the areas of literature and social science. The student must be looked at as an individual when recommending adult literature to him.

As librarians think of students as gifted, average, disadvantaged, or reluctant readers, it is easy to stereotype them, while in reality each is an individual who must be accepted where he is and led to a satisfying experience.

Just as individual guidance in reading is given, so does the library staff provide assistance in selecting materials for listening and viewing. Students must be guided to think naturally of all kinds of media as means of acquiring knowledge. In addition, they must be aided in their realization of when audiovisual materials complement printed ones, when one form is better than another depending on the present purpose.

Orientation

Guidance by the library staff varies widely from a simple pointing out of the location of certain materials to special help for a hard-to-solve request. Some guidance takes the form of a program of teaching students how to use the library. Apart from teaching library usage is orientation to the library. All students new to a school need simple orientation in the location of materials in that particular library, an introduction to its regulations, and the kinds of services available. In a three-year high school, all tenth graders must have this orientation sometime during the first few weeks of the school year. Although often done through their English classes, it can be equally well accomplished during the time alloted to school activities. Library orientation may be in the form of one or more locally-produced filmstrips, as is done at Arizona State University. It is a good idea to give each student a simple floor plan with the following things marked: listening area, viewing area, audiovisual materials, Reader's Guide and other periodical indexes, circulation desk, reference area, vertical files, magazines (current and back issues), card catalog, staff offices, books of fiction, non-fiction and special collections. Students must then look around the library to locate these areas. A single sheet listing the library's services and specific rules is also given to the students, with opportunity allowed for students to ask questions. When schools have handbooks for new students including this kind of library information, these separate sheets are not necessary. However, opportunity must still be given for students to become familiar with the location of library equipment and materials in the early weeks of their high school career.

The student in any or all grades who transfers into a school at any time during the school year must not be neglected in library orientation. When the library is one of the places in the school which receives the schedule card of every student, the library immediately knows who these students are. Through using an invitation form, individual appointments for them to come to the library for orientation can be arranged. When there is a large and frequent influx of new students, this orientation may be best accomplished by group appointments on a regular monthly basis. For example, all of the students who arrive at the school in one particular month can meet in the library during the activity period of the last school day of that month.

Teaching Students Library Use

Teaching students how to use the library is an important part of the library's services. It is entirely separate from the orientation needed by new students. Students' needs vary widely, depending on their prior library experiences and their general familiarity with books and other materials. At the secondary level, teaching the use of the library is accomplished best when it is incorporated with a specific need and when it is done on an individual and small group basis. Students attending schools in a community where the elementary schools have taught things which are common to most libraries--whether public or school or college--and have put their knowledge into practice, will have a strong foundation on which to base their secondary school library experiences. Such basic library learnings include: the parts of a book; how to operate simple projectors and recorders; the arrangement and shelving of books, pamphlets, records, films and other material; the location of materials through the card catalog or printed catalogs; the use and purpose of certain reference books; library vocabulary. Hopefully, through frequent use, these points are learned well so that they are very familiar. They will also have been exposed to certain social learnings such as the care of public property, neatness and sharing with others. Other students will have limited knowledge and experience in libraries so that they will have to be taught most elementary aspects of a library. In either case, librarians and teachers know that library knowledge is often not retained as well as other subjects, and therefore must be repeated by a variety of means. By means of a brief questionnaire to a group of students, it can be assertained just how much each one knows today. The use of professionally prepared, standardized tests such as those listed at the end of this chapter can be considered. When it appears that the majority of the sophomore class needs basic training in library usage, probably it is best to schedule these students through a subject class which they all take. Those students in each class who are immediately identified through the test or through adroit questioning to have a little more knowledge than the others, can be used as assistants to their fellow students along with their teacher and the librarian as the lessons progress. Regardless of how few or how many sessions are held for teaching the use of the library, they must be incorporated with or followed by an actual class lesson. An assignment to study the lives of people is an example of a good follow-up to library instruction which can be used in any and every area of the curriculum. Biography in itself has the further advantage of appealing to teenagers, as they like to identify with other people. Any school librarian can testify to the popularity of biographies for personal reading. Furthermore, biography makes a good follow-up exercise because it can involve the use of all kinds of media, including books of fiction and non-fiction, reference books, magazines, pamphlets, pictures, recordings by and about the biographee, films and filmstrips. It also has the advantage that each member of the class can study a different individual. As the assignment is completed, the librarian and the teacher share responsibility for looking over the presentations to see what knowledge concerning the library has been gained. Library lessons which are not tied up with a classroom assignment will seem to be abstract and uninteresting. They may also be largely a matter of talking or demonstration by the library staff. This accomplishes very little when we remember that direct participation is a large part of the learning process.

By far the most effective library teaching in the high school is done when students need it, frequently in curriculum related assignments. As teachers make such plans for their students, they come to the library to talk over the wide variety of ways in which this is accomplished, depending on the nature of the assignment and its length of duration. One of the ways most practiced is to bring the class to the library. Here some time may be spent on pointing out all of the kinds of library materials useful for the assignment. A review of certain techniques may be given as needed, using the students' topics as examples. Extra catalog cards which the library has on the general subject being studied can be distributed to everyone in the class. The librarian can use the overhead projector to point out how cards for books, films, recordings, etc., differ from each other and the kinds of information found on catalog cards. Posters explaining the two ways of alphabetizing as found in different reference books can be shown. When the assignment involves the study of a particular subject, the library classification scheme for that subject can be given to the students in bookmark form. The use of games easily adaptable to special needs is a good way to get across the information. Commercially produced filmstrips and slides on encyclopedias, the _Reader's Guide_, special reference books and the card catalog are useful. But care must be taken to be sure that there are not so many exceptions to local practice in a particular filmstrip as to make its use confusing to the students. Some schools produce their own library filmstrips and transparencies.

The subject of instruction in the use of libraries was included in the 1963 American Library Association conference on "An Inquiry into the Needs of Students, Libraries, and the Educational Process."[4] The inadequacy of many local schools' efforts and the waste of duplicate efforts was pointed out. Joseph L. Wheeler has outlined a proposal expanding this idea through instruction for college students and adults as well as school children and young people.[5] He suggests that a group of materials be carefully worked out by professional people under the direction of the American Library Association with the possibility of financial backing by the Federal Government or a foundation. A variety of attractive and carefully prepared and designed printed materials which include descriptions of various information tools, facsimilies of pages from these tools, and pictures of them being used are needed. Pamphlets or loose-leaf sheets making library tools applicable for each high school subject are proposed. Mr. Wheeler also suggests the preparation of audiovisual materials on a variety of problems and different approaches to the library.

Time must be given for putting into practice things learned about the library. The precise nature of the practice and the amount of time needed will vary. It is a good idea for students to work in pairs or small groups so that they can help each other, the goal being success for every member of the class. Those students who obviously know more than the others should be placed with different groups so that their knowledge can be spread around. The teacher and the library staff are always there to assist as needed during these practice sessions. Just how much time a class spends in the library depends on the nature of the assignment and the previous experiences of that particular group of students. The entire class may continue to come to the library on a pre-arranged schedule until the assignment is completed, or the library visit may be simply for introduction to the work which students will be expected to complete on their own time and at their own convenience. The teachers may have an understanding with the library staff that a few students will be coming to the library from time to time during the class period to work independently on their library assignment.

As the teaching of library use is incorporated with other class assignments, reference is made to knowledge gained on previous class visits to the library. Frequent repetition of library techniques as applicable to each need reinforces the learning, so that students become very familiar with the library and are made quickly aware of possibilities of the cross-media approach to their needs.

For a good library program as related to the curriculum, there must be constant communication between teachers and librarians. As teachers become aware of individual needs of their students, they see to it that the library staff is informed. In schools where students are scheduled into one or more of their classes according to their ability, this fact must be taken into account as library instruction is given. It is easy to assume that students in college preparatory classes are more familiar with libraries than those in standard or remedial classes. This is not necessarily so, as their experiences may have been very limited. However, it is likely that they will learn more quickly than the others. The amount and kind of library instruction given varies considerably, depending on the construction of the curriculum in a particular school and the varying abilities of the students.

The needs of the college-bound student for greater library knowledge are shown in a study made in 1960.[6] In answer to the question of what the weaknesses are in secondary school preparation for doing college assignments requiring the use of the library, professors and librarians from one hundred colleges listed the following points as the most frequent weaknesses:

1. Inability to use the card catalog in the college library effectively and to the fullest extent. Students are especially weak in reference to the subject approach and they do not know how to make full use of the information contained on catalog cards.

2. Unfamiliarity with use of indexes, especially indexes other than Reader's Guide.

3. Apparent lack of practice in library usage and elementary research procedures.

4. Inability to 'pursue the search' for material and information if it is not found quickly and readily. Some respondents said, 'Too easy dependence on the librarian.'

5. Inexperience or complete inability in compiling bibliographies and making footnote references.

It is easy for librarians to think of library instruction as an end in itself. When audiovisual aids are used in this instruction, there seems to be an even greater danger to think of it in this way. But the real goals of locating and gathering together materials are the evaluation, appreciation, or thought stimulus which results from such an undertaking.

Librarian Visits Classes

The role of the librarian as counselor and teacher is not confined to the library area. Taking a group of materials into a classroom at the request of the teacher is common practice. They may include magazines, books, filmstrips, records, paperbacks to be sold, or only one or two of these materials. They may have been chosen from the library jointly by teacher and librarian, or the teacher may have sent a committee from her class to do the selecting. These materials may be left in the classroom on short-term loan, they may be checked out to individual students sometime during the period, or returned to the library to be placed on reserve for the duration of their use by that particular class. The librarian visits the classroom to publicize new library materials related to that class, to talk about personal libraries and many other subjects.

Developing Self-Reliance

Whether librarians or teachers have actual responsibility for teaching study skills, librarians have a good opportunity to notice students' study habits. In addition, students' ability to take notes and to follow through on using library materials is observed. The librarian must give help as needed and make note of the extent to which further group instruction is required. The problem of when to stop leading the student by the hand as he attempts library assignments is a challenging one to the librarian. Should librarians, themselves, locate the needed materials quickly and simply lay them out on the table, so that the student can spend all of his time absorbing them for his use? Self-reliance is developed in many ways as the teen-ager grows toward adulthood. An important part of the education process is becoming independent learners. Some students will never be able to understand or need to know how to use the syntopican accompanying the Encyclopaedia Britannica's Great Books of the Western World. Some will go far beyond that, as they absorb the wealth of material available. A few may gain no more than a feeling that the library is a friendly place where they are welcome. Independent, self-reliant library use, to the extent possible by each student, is a major goal of the entire library guidance program.

Orientation and guidance are not confined to students. Teachers new to a school need time for library orientation prior to the first day of school. A couple of hours spent in the library getting acquainted with materials and services and talking with the library staff is necessary.

Teacher Training and Libraries

Something must be said about the education of teachers in the use of the library. The reason why certain teachers never or seldom make library assignments may well be because they, themselves, know very little about the contents of the library or how to use it. Very few colleges and universities incorporate this kind of training for all of their students; nor do they make it a part of their teacher-education program. In a study made by the National Education Association in 1960, it was revealed that 86.9% of the teachers studied had no training in how libraries could be used in their teaching. Perkins made an interesting study in this area of college seniors who were preparing to be teachers.[7] After making a pilot survey of 298 college seniors to discover what problems would arise in using standardized tests for larger groups, 4000 students from sixty-nine colleges were given the Peabody Library Information Test or the _Library Orientation Test for College Freshmen._ Of those who took the Peabody Test, only 74 percent recognized an author card as such, and about three-fourths did not know what the general coverage of the _Reader's Guide_ was. Most of the results were so bad that the conclusion was reached that prospective teachers know little about libraries and that the libraries in today's colleges and universities are being wasted. Incorporated into the education of prospective teachers must be methods of using the library in their teaching.

The move away from the single text to multiple sources of learning has been going on at all levels for many years. Not only are multiple texts used but many library materials of all kinds. Schools may prepare their own materials as well as buy them. When this is the case, the local school or school district plans inservice training or workshops for its teachers in how to plan and make transparencies, slides, filmstrips and films. Such sessions are necessary particularly when teachers have received little or no information in their formal college education. Whether or not it is better to buy commercially produced audiovisual materials must be thoroughly considered before a school goes into the production of these materials. Even when a school buys most of its audiovisual aids, there should be provision for the making of simple transparencies, charts and posters. In addition, various machines for duplicating material must be available. There is also the possibility of having people on the school's staff who are employed to do the work of producing materials at a teacher's request. Probably this arrangement is best, because the expert knowledge needed in producing many materials cannot be gained adequately in inservice training or workshop sessions. But in any case, the production of materials is administered by the library and is a part of its service. The high school teacher of every subject needs to know what the school library contains in his subject area and the nature and extent of the services he can expect from the library staff. The planning of informal training sessions by the library staff to demonstrate the possible ways in which material can be used is a necessity. Librarians constantly need to show teachers new materials. They need to explain the use of certain reference books.

The writer experimented with making appointments with individual teachers in a high school where she was the librarian. The following simple form was sent to the teacher:

VHS Library Date_________

To:

From: Helen E. Saunders, Librarian

Will you please come to the library on _________ _________during your conference period ( ) in order to see some of the materials which are available for your classroom assignments.

Although the meeting began with looking at materials, other factors were frequently brought into the conference, such as the needs of certain students whom the teacher had in class and what the library could do for them, ways to use library materials in a particular study, the availability of professional materials for the teacher. When it was possible to work it out, these appointments turned into small group conferences particularly of teachers who taught the same subject.

As librarians go about the task of helping to meet the needs of students and teachers through expert guidance, their role in teaching and guiding the individual becomes apparent.

Notes

1. G. Robert Carlsen, "For Everything There is a Season," Top of the News, XXI (January, 1965), 103-110.

2. Scope, Scholastic Magazines, Inc., 902 Sylvan Ave., Englewood Cliffs, New Jersey. 07632

3. John Rowell, "Pennsylvania--More Bears than Books," ALA Bulletin, LVIII (October, 1964), 816+

4. Lowell Martin, "Lowell Martin's CWC Survey," ALA Bulletin LVII (September, 1963), 739.

5. Joseph L. Wheeler, "Project: Instruction in Use of Books and Libraries from First Grade to Old Age, Nationally," The Author, Benson, Vermont. 05731

6. "What Should College Freshmen Know about the Library," Library Journal, LXXXV (February 15, 1960), 828.

7. Ralph Perkins, The Prospective Teacher's Knowledge of Library Fundamentals... The Scarecrow Press, Inc., 1965.

Selected Audiovisual Materials

General Guidance

* Library Art of Guidance. 16mm film. sound, black and white, 8 min. 1965. Dr. Margaret E. Monroe, Consultant. Bureau of Audio-Visual Instruction, University of Wisconsin, Madison, Wisconsin. 53706

* School Libraries in Action. 16mm film. sound, color, 18 min. 1960. Cora Paul Bomar, State Supervisor, School Library Services, Department of Public Instruction, Raleigh, N.C. 27602

Teenagers Will Read. 16mm film. color, 27 min. n.d. AV Education Center, University of Michigan, Ann Arbor, Michigan. 48106

Why Johnny Reads Junk. 16mm film. sound, black and white, 29 min. 1959. National Educational Television Film Service, AV Center, Indiana University, Bloomington, Indiana. 47405

Instruction in the Use of the Library

* Card Catalog. Filmstrip. 51 frames, color, recorded script (33 1/3 rpm) Library Filmstrip Center, 14 N. Old Manor, Wichita, Kansas. 67208

Developing a Science Fair Project. Filmstrip. 50 frames, color, recorded script (33 1/3 rpm) 1967. Library Filmstrip Center.

Finding Facts and Figures. Filmstrip. 32 frames, color, 1962. (Advanced English Series) Filmstrip House, 432 Park Ave. South, New York, N.Y. 10016

* Library. Set of 3 filmstrips. color, 1961. Essential Education, Box 968 Huntsville, Texas 77340
Making the Library a Learning Center. 40 frames
Using the Library for Research. 40 frames
Cooperating with the Librarian. 37 frames

* Reader's Guide, Ready Reference. Filmstrip. 47 frames, color, recorded script (33 1/3 rpm) 1963. Library Filmstrip Center.

The Reference Collection. Filmstrip. 50 frames, color, recorded script (33 1/3 rpm) Library Filmstrip Center.

The Research Paper. Filmstrip. 47 frames, color, recorded script (33 1/3 rpm) Library Filmstrip Center.

* The University Library. 16mm film. sound, color, 25 min., n.d. Yale University Alumni Board. Association Instructional Materials, 600 Madison Ave., New York, N. Y. 10022

Using the Library to Improve Class Reports. Set of 3 filmstrips.

color. 1962. Guidance Filmstrips, Box 63, Houston, Texas. 77001

* You and Your Library. 16mm film. sound, color, 11 min. 1962. C-B Educational Films, 12 Geary St., San Francisco, Calif. 94108

Inservice Training in the Use of Audiovisual Materials

* Demonstration Tape for Teachers. Tape. 3 3/4 speed; side 1 - 40 min.; side 2 - 26 min. n. d.

Facts about Projection. (Audio-Visual Training Series) 16mm film. sound, color, 16 min. 1959. International Film Bureau, 332 S. Michigan, Chicago, Illinois. 60604

Filmstrips and the Teacher. (Using Audiovisual Materials Series) Filmstrip. 45 frames, color. 1962. McGraw-Hill Textfilms, 330 W. 42nd St., New York, N.Y. 10036

Instructional Materials. (Professional Education Series) Filmstrip. 44 frames, color. 1961. Bel Mort Films, 619 Cascade Bldg., Portland, Oregon. 97200

How the teacher selects and uses all types of instructional materials for different purposes.

New Dimensions through Teaching Films. 16mm film. sound, color, 28 min. 1963. Coronet Instructional Films, 65 East S. Walter, Chicago, Illinois. 60601

Selection and Use of Programmed Materials. Filmstrip. 64 frames, color. 1964. Includes script, handbook, record. Division of Audiovisual Instruction, National Education Association, 1201 Sixteenth St. N.W., Washington, D.C. 20036

Teaching Machines. (Automated Teaching Series) Filmstrip. Basic Skill Films, 1355 Inverness Drive, Pasadena, California. 91102

* Available on loan for payment of round-trip shipping costs from Headquarters Library, American Library Association, 50 East Huron St., Chicago, Illinois. 60611. In the case of films, there is also a three-dollar fee.

Selected Readings

Guidance to Meet Specific Needs

Batchelor, Lillian L., ed. Reading Guidance for the Gifted. 1960 Library Institute Proceedings. Los Angeles, California: Immaculate Heart College, 1960.

Beringhausen, D. K. and R. W. Faunce. "Exploratory Study of Juvenile Delinquency and the Reading of Sensational Books," Journal of Experimental Education, XXXIII (Winter, 1964), 161-168.

Boutwell, W. D. "Motivating the Slow Learner," Wilson Library Bulletin, XL (September, 1965), 75-77.

Carlsen, G. Robert. Books and the Teenage Reader. Published simultaneously by Bantam Books and Harper and Row, 1967.

Ideas for library programs for teenagers. Also lists over 700 selected titles.

__________. "The Right Size," Top of the News, XXIII (November, 1966), 55-62.

Discussion of the interests of teenagers in relation to what they read.

Cleary, Florence D. Blueprints for Better Reading... New York: The H. W. Wilson Co., 1957.

In spite of the publication date, this book has fine ideas applicable today for reading guidance.

Edwards, Margaret. "A Time and Season for the Better Reader," Top of the News, XXI (April, 1965), 229-235.

Galbraith, John K. "Let's Don't be too Solemn about Books," ALA Bulletin, LIX (February, 1965), 112-114.

Knudson, Rozanne. "To Corrupt? To Enoble? To Anything? The Impact of Reading as Described by School Librarians," California School Libraries, XXXVIII (January, 1967), 9-12.

Kvaraceus, William C. "Can Reading Affect Delinquency?" ALA Bulletin, LIX (June, 1965), 516-522.

Lee, Elsie J. "Serving the Gifted," School Libraries, XIII (May, 1964), 11-17.

Magaliff, Cecile. The Junior Novel; its Relationship to Adolescent Reading. Port Washington, New York: Kennikat Press, 1964.

Miller, Leonard M. *Guidance for the Under-achiever with Superior Ability.* (Bulletin 1961, No. 25) Washington, D. C.: U. S. Government Printing Office, 1961.

"Providing School Library Service for the Culturally Disadvantaged." A reprint of articles appearing in the *ALA Bulletin*, June 1964-January 1965. Printed for the American Association of School Librarians.

Includes an annotated bibliography.

Smith, Sister Raphael Mary. "A Study of the Reading Interests of Ninth Grade Girls in Selected American and Canadian Schools as Reflected in their Choice of Free Reading." M.A. in L.S. Thesis, Immaculate Heart College, 1962.

Trezise, Joan Lenon. "Plan for Critical Reading," *School Libraries*, XIV (May, 1965), 31-32.

A plan for teaching ninth graders who are superior readers to "read beyond the plot."

Walker, Richard D. "The Influence of Antecedent Library Service upon Academic Achievement of University of Illinois Freshmen." Ph.D. Thesis, University of Illinois, 1963.

Available on microfilm from University Microfilms, Ann Arbor, Michigan. 48106

"Working with Disadvantaged Young Adults." Working papers prepared for the ALA's Young Adult Services Division institute on library services for disadvantaged youth, July 8-10, 1966. The Division, American Library Association.

Eight reports including: library programs for disadvantaged youth, non-book materials, popular paperbacks, rural library services, library working with other community agencies.

Instruction in the Use of the Library

Henne, Frances. "Learning to Learn in School Libraries," *School Libraries*, XV (May, 1966), 15-23.

Hopkinson, Shirley L. *Instructional Materials for Teaching the Use of the Library.* San Jose, California: Claremont House, 1966. (pamphlet) Order from the author, 231 E. San Fernando, San Jose, California. 95112

Extensive selected and annotated bibliography of all kinds of media. For all levels, primary through adult.

Johnson, Alice E. "Library Instruction 'En Masse'," *School Libraries*, XI (January, 1962), 21-23+

Moon, Eric. "Pre-Conference Potpourri: AV Showtime," Library Journal, XCI (August, 1966), 3640-3642.

Library orientation programs.

Sayles, Lois. "Teaching Library Skills Through Subject Matter," Education, LXXXVI (March, 1966), 412-415.

Instruction in the Use of the Library: Handbooks and Other Aids

Biermann, Lillian M. Your Library: How to Use it. New York: Harper and Row, 1962.

Text-workbook containing 18 lessons, the first 9 of which are designed to be taught as a unit. Flexible program for use by teachers and librarians in junior high schools.

Cleary, Florence D. Discovering Books and Libraries: A Handbook for the Upper Elementary and Junior High School Grades. New York: The H. W. Wilson Co., 1966.

Conlon, Eileen. Books Lead the Way: Library and Reading Skills Text. New York: The Scarecrow Press, Inc., 1964.

Practical book containing more than 40 exercises and activities for use with students grades 4 through 9. Also available to accompany the above: Manual for Teachers and Librarians.

How to Use the Library Program Book. Programed by MLI Associates. Boston: Allyn and Bacon, Inc., 1966.

This programed text for junior and senior high school use allows each student to proceed at his own rate in gaining library knowledge. Three kinds of frames are used: teaching, review, laboratory. Accompanied by: How to Use the Library Exhibit Book.

Rossoff, Martin. Using your High School Library. 2d ed. New York: The H. W. Wilson Co., 1964.

Shankman, F. V. and R. Kranyik. How to Teach Reference and Research Skills. (Prentice-Hall Education Series) Englewood Cliffs, New Jersey: Teachers Practical Press, Inc., 1964.

Sturgis Enlarged Catalog Cards. Sturgis, Michigan: Library Products, Inc. Set of 19 Wilson cards enlarged to 22" x 14".

Toser, Marie A. Library Manual: a Study-Work Manual of Lessons on the Use of Books and Libraries. 6th ed. New York: The H. W. Wilson Co., 1964.

Ten units of lessons for junior and senior high school students. Separate envelope of examination questions. Teacher's Key available.

Instruction in the Use of the Library: Standardized Tests

Bennett, Alma and H. W. Schrammel. *Bennett Use of Library Test. High School and College.* Emporia, Kansas: Bureau of Educational Measurements, Kansas State Teachers College, 1947.

Feagley, Ethel and others. *A Library Orientation Test for College Freshmen.* New York: Bureau of Publications, Teachers College, Columbia University, 1955.

Test on the Use of Books and Libraries: General Education Series. Grades 7-12. Princeton, New Jersey: Cooperative Test Division, Educational Testing Service, 1950.

Use of Sources of Information: Iowa Tests of Educational Development. Test 9. Grades 9-13. Chicago: Science Research Associates, 1951.

Inservice Training in the Use of Audiovisual Materials

Facts you Should Know about Filmstrips. San Fernando, California: Frank Holmes Laboratories, Inc., 1965.

Gerlach, V. S. *Audiovisual Equipment and Procedures Manual.* Tempe, Arizona: Arizona State University, 1966.

Kemp, Jerrold E. *Planning and Producing Audiovisual Materials.* San Francisco: Chandler Publishing Co., 1963.

Limbacher, James L. "Film Evaluation and Criticism," *ALA Bulletin*, LVIII (January, 1964), 43-48.

Meierhenry, W. C. *Media Competencies for Teachers.* Lincoln, Nebraska: Teachers College, University of Nebraska, 1966.

Minor, Ed. *Simplified Techniques for Preparing Audio-Visual Instructional Materials.* New York: McGraw-Hill Book Co., 1962.

Teacher Education and the Library

McIntosh, Marethal B. and Stacy Hall. "Student Teachers in the School Library," *School Libraries*, XII (March, 1963), 43-47.

Walker, Jerry L. "What do Student Teachers Know about Libraries?" *School Libraries*, XVI (Winter, 1967), 17-18+

Witt, Paul W. F. "Teacher Education and School Libraries," *School Libraries*, XIV (October, 1964), 37-46.

Chapter III

The Use of the Library: Some General Considerations

"The most important part of the library program is work with students and teachers, those activities and services that make the library an educational force in the school."[1] Thus the Standards for School Library Programs states directly and simply the chief purpose of the school library. If the library is to be an educational force, it must have an on-going program of meaningful activities both within the library and elsewhere, which directly affects all teachers and students. In accordance with the school's philosophy, this program includes: guidance to meet individual, personal and social needs; growth in library skills; and assistance in study and research as related to the curriculum. The extent to which such a program exists depends on the nature of the quantitative standards in four areas: funds, materials, personnel, quarters. In many communities, high standards have only recently been met. In others, increasing recognition of the part played by the library in the total school program has caused existing standards to be raised in all four areas. In either case, careful planning and frequent evaluation for a period of years is likely to be necessary before the ideal is met. As standards are considered, it is important to remember all four aspects. If a school spends ten dollars per pupil for materials but has no adequate place to house them, their use will be limited. No matter how large a collection of carefully selected materials a library purchases, if there is not adequate personnel to administer them, maximum use will not be attained. All quantitative standards for funds, materials, personnel, and quarters are not ends in themselves. They are a necessary means to the goal of maximum library service for the entire school.

Teacher-made Assignments

A large part of library service in the secondary school is

through assignments made by teachers. There are many factors to be considered as teachers make these library-related assignments for their students. Consideration is given to relating the assignment to the abilities of the students, so that the same assignment is adapted to the accelerated, the standard and the remedial. Library materials are ideal sources of meeting individual needs. Each title in the library's book collection is different from the one next to it. Some have vocabularies for the adult reader, while others on the same subject are written with the vocabulary of the average elementary school child. Many magazines and newspapers are available for use by the student whose span of attention is short, regardless of how well or how poorly he reads. Films, recordings, and other non-print library materials can be adapted to meet individual needs in the same way as printed materials. In addition, audiovisual aids have a unique appeal in themselves, which makes their occasional or frequent use mandatory.

Obtaining Ideas

Some ideas as to ways in which library materials can be incorporated with classroom programs must be acquired. In addition to activities and readings found in many textbooks, the regular reading of professional periodicals leads teachers to new ideas. As teachers attend meetings and conferences, locally and otherwise, they see materials and obtain ideas which they want to try with their own students. Since librarians often have access to all kinds of publications and resources in many fields not usually available to teachers, the school library staff is a fine source of ideas. The substitution of other texts for those students who find the assigned ones too difficult or too easy may result in the use of library books. As the teacher learns more about the abilities of his students, he finds ways--often through library materials--to have his students work to their maximum capacity. In attempting to make the subject attractive--and consequently the learning easier--the teacher uses the library.

Contents of the Library

Another consideration is the amount and kind of material which the library contains. A library which has had an annual budget of five dollars or more per pupil for general library books plus additional amounts for films, recordings, filmstrips, magazines, newspapers, and special reference books over a period of years will certainly have a large collection of material. Hopefully they have been carefully selected to meet the needs of the curriculum and of the individuals in that particular school, and that outdated materials have been removed from time to time. It is unfortunately true that far too many school libraries do not contain either enough materials or a good working collection to meet the demands of today's curriculum. There is a great deal of "catching up" to be done, necessitating the expenditures of large sums of money for materials and the hiring of professional librarians, all of whom as a part of their education have learned the importance of wise and careful selection of materials. Ideally the teacher can expect to find materials adequate both in kind and number for the use of his students, but unfortunately he cannot take this for granted. When teachers go ahead and make library assignments without checking to see what materials are available, they are bound to be disappointed in the results which may ensue. The students themselves become frustrated when adequate materials are not available for a particular need, and they also become annoyed with the library for not having materials which they are required to use. Some teachers tell their students that if the school library doesn't have the needed information, to go to the public library. This only compounds the problem. The public library may or may not have the material. When it does, it may very well be in circulation, considering that the public library serves the entire community. Students should always have available a good library in their school to meet curriculum-related requirements. Not only must the library have the materials they need but students must be given some class time to go to the library, or materials must be available in the classroom. When there are no proper materials in the school library or no time is allowed for their use, students have a legitimate reason for not getting a library assignment.

How is the Library Used Best?

The amount of time to be given for completing the assignment is another factor in making library assignments, as are the details of how the library is to be used. The solution to these particular factors depends on the nature of the assignment and how much help the students need. Some assignments are best met by materials being put on reserve for the use of a particular class during the two or three weeks' duration of the assignment. Others need an introductory visit to the library. Some will be accomplished best with regular sessions in the library, where the teacher of the class and the library staff give the necessary help, during the length of time decided upon for the library study. In some cases a good deal of teaching and guidance in library fundamentals will be required before the actual class assignment can be started. Sometimes half of a class may need more than the usual assistance from the teacher in order to get even a minimum from the regular lessons, while the rest of the class is made up of gifted students who do the daily work quickly and easily. A good plan is to arrange with the library staff to send this latter group to the library during the class period for enrichment projects, while the teacher works closely in the classroom with the other students.

Successful Library Experiences

Basic to all successful library experiences is communication and understanding between teachers and librarians. They must work as a team in planning and carrying out every assignment involving library materials. Some teachers may feel that the whole process sounds too complicated and is more work than it is worth. The library staff must endeavor to dispell this idea by suggesting that all of the foregoing considerations are not to be thought of in relation to every library activity. Encouraging every student in a history class, for instance, to find a library book he is willing to read is a perfectly satisfactory goal and one fairly easy to accomplish, when guidance from teacher and librarians is available in a well stocked library. Teachers need to be encouraged to try different techniques, knowing that what succeeds with some students fails with others.

List of Suggestions for Use of Library

Librarians frequently list suggestions to teachers as to ways in which the library can be used by their students, together with a form which can be checked and returned to the library. Here follows an example of such a list and form.

"The Library Gives the Student an Opportunity to Succeed on Whatever Level He Is"

1. Visit the library for the selection of books for free reading in your subject.

2. Visit the library for the selection of books on a central theme. Examples: Pioneer life, the family in fiction, primitive man, modern furniture. These themes might correspond with units in a textbook. A committee of students could set aside these books ahead of time.

3. Visit the library for magazine browsing. If this is to be something more than an exercise in magazine-thumbing, the following follow-up procedures are suggested: (a) ask students to evaluate one of several periodicals, (b) ask them to analyze contents of a favorite magazine, (c) bring back to class a report on some article of interest.

4. When assigning papers, begin with a visit to the library for: (a) the selection of a subject, (b) discovering availability of material, (c) making a tentative bibliography.

5. Visit the library to select material for panel discussions on current and controversial subjects.

6. Have a committee of students look over the library's collection in your subject in order to select 30 or 40 books to take to the classroom to "sell" to the students.

7. Ask the librarian to make a bibliography of the books our library has on a given topic.

8. Displays in the library of classroom projects such as: notebooks, scrapbooks, models.

Teacher-Request Form Valley High School

To the Librarian: Date ____________

I. I am interested in having my _____ (number) classes in ______________ (subject) visit the library for the purpose of ____________________________________.
I would like to have them come ________________
__________________ (Give 1st and 2nd choice of

dates) during Periods ______________________.

II. I am assigning ___________(number) students in ________(number) classes the following subject: __________________________. They will need the material from ___________ to ___________. It is understood that this material will be placed on reserve for my students, to be used only in the library or borrowed overnight. It will be shelved at the Reference Desk.

III. I am assigning_____(number) classes to write papers on ______________________________.
They are due ______________________________.
Limitations as to number and kind of references to be used:______________________________.

IV. Please select some books for extra reading on the following subject:______________________.
Put them on a special shelf for_______________ (name of course) to be borrowed by my students for the regular two-weeks period.

____
Teacher's signature

It is a good idea for the librarian to list certain practical points for teachers who are planning class visits to the library. The following could be included:

1. Arrangements for classes or parts of classes to visit the library must be made at least 48 hours in advance.

2. Some comment on the purpose of the library visit, assignment of topics (if necessary), conduct in library, etc., should be made before the visit.

3. Roll call, announcements, etc., should be taken care of before the class comes to the library.

4. If an entire class is visiting the library, it should be accompanied by the teacher who will remain during the entire period.

5. A maximum of half the members of a class can be sent to the library unaccompanied by the teacher, provided the students are from the upper level of the class.

____
Head Librarian's Signature

As teachers and librarians plan carefully together, there is more chance for satisfactory library experiences.

How can the library be used successfully? Described here are three common ways in which the library is used successfully in every area of the curriculum: free reading on the subject, biographies of people in the area, careers in the field.

Free Reading

The purpose of free reading is two-fold. Since students sometimes have the idea that all books are texts and that texts have all of the answers, free reading gives them a chance to discover the wealth and variety of material written on a subject. The other major purpose is to find out that the subject is a "live" one on which materials are constantly being written. The teacher and the library staff may select the materials for free reading, being sure that there is a large number to choose from. The teacher may bring the class to the library or the librarian may take the materials to the classroom. In either case, the librarian makes brief comments about some of the books. He may give the students a sheet of paper containing the major Dewey classification numbers and popular subject headings found in the card catalog as they relate to the subject. In order that this activity be more than a "thumbing" exercise, students may be asked to make a brief evaluation of the book or magazine, or to describe its contents. At the end of the period, students are able to check out any of the materials if they want to.

Biography

Since the lives of people are usually of considerable interest to all ages, a study of biography can be a valuable and satisfying library assignment. Recordings of speeches by famous people are good to use. Pictures of leaders in the field are displayed. The librarian introduces biographical reference books and leads a discussion of the difference between the treatment of a person's life in reference tools and in regular books of biography.

Careers

A study of careers in a field is an interesting part of many courses in the secondary school. In some subjects of the curriculum, it will be best to widen this study into related areas. For example, a class in typing can study jobs as a file clerk, receptionist, office machine operator, and secretary, as well as that of typist. The use of pamphlets are valuable in a study of careers, as they are apt to contain more up-to-date information. Charts listing a comparison of salaries with other occupations can be used. Films showing people at work in the field can add to the interest. A major part of the study of careers can be an investigation of post-high school education. In fields where college education and graduate training are necessary, this part of the study can be quite thorough and detailed, including potential cost, scholarship possibilities, etc.

Just about any teacher who tries one or more of the preceeding types of assignments will find that they are apt to be successful, when the groundwork is laid in cooperation with the library staff.

Notes

1. American Association of School Librarians, _op. cit._, p. 7.

Chapter IV

Library Services to the Various Academic Disciplines

English Department

Since English is a required course during all years in most secondary schools, the library must contain a large and varied collection of materials for the use of students of English.

A good example of library involvement in the English class is demonstrated in the study of mythology as presented by Mrs. Diane Campbell, seventh grade English teacher at Farrer Junior High School in Provo, Utah. The outline for her study is given here.

Mythology Unit Outline

This unit is designed to teach library skills plus give the student an introduction to the vast subject of mythology. The student studies one story in depth and reports on it to the class and hears the other stories told by other students. This unit can be made as simple or as complex as the teacher wants and needs. The following is a brief outline which is very flexible. Material can be added or deleted to make it conform to the interests and capabilities of the students.

I. Introduction
   A. Show common references to mythology - trademarks, pictures, headlines, etc.
   B. Give students a chance to identify and explain references to class. (Extra credit could be given for finding other references, identifying them, and bringing to class.)
   C. Give list of spelling words with mythological background.
   D. Explain how each word relates to mythology.
      1. Use transparencies (if possible).
      2. Have students look up words and report to class.

II. Research report
   A. Hand out lists of topics.
   B. Assign topic (Use any method desired).
   C. Give students list of research requirements. (These can be as simple or as complex as the teacher desires.)

   D. Allow sufficient time in library for research (one-two weeks).
   E. Have students hand in completed papers.

III. Oral reports
   A. Before handing in reports students will need to make a short outline of story.
   B. Each student puts his outline on the board for other students to take notes.
   C. The student tells story or about character to class.
   D. Two-part test given.
      1. Test from memory on Olympians, asking Greek and Roman names and major realm.
      2. Test using notes from introduction and student notes.

The mythology study lasted for a period of approximately five weeks, during which time the class went to the library as needed for research. Although all seventh graders at Farrer had three days of library orientation at the beginning of the year, they needed a good deal of assistance from the library staff as they began their research. Using the faculty workroom which adjoins the school library, the teacher made transparencies on mythology, adapting some described in a publication of the Channing L. Bete Company on a Scriptographic Unit of Knowledge. Appropriate tapes and phono-records were borrowed from the library for classroom use. Attractive posters illustrating various myths were made by the students and displayed in the classroom and in the school's halls. The library staff made lists of the books available in the library. These lists as well as attractive "mythology" bookmarks were distributed to each student. During the study, a videotape was made showing the highlights of the classroom and library sessions. This contributed to the evaluation of the project by the teacher, the library staff, and the students.

This study involved careful planning by a teacher who had an idea and who was willing to do a good deal of work to carry it out. It is obvious that cooperation from the library staff was necessary. But there was nothing about the study which made it too difficult or unusual for any teacher to undertake.

Tape recordings made by authors reading their own works is a kind of library material commonly used by teachers of English.

An interesting variation of these recordings are ones which are interviews with authors. One such group of tapes is the result of questions asked of certain writers including Dr. Irving Adler, Pearl S. Buck, Elizabeth Enright, Fred Gipson, and Phyllis Whitney, by school children.[1]

The value of paperbacks for use by students of English was the subject of a national survey in 1960 by the National Council of Teachers of English.[2] Teachers felt that paperbacks are apt to increase the students' interest in reading. In addition, the teachers noted that the comparatively low cost of paperbacks and their easy availability makes it possible for many students to build a personal library.

Social Studies Department

The use of the library by the social studies department is essential for good teaching and learning. A bewildering variety of books and audiovisual materials is available in the social studies field. It is impossible to pick up a book reviewing magazine which does not contain reviews of one or more new history books. This wealth of material makes their selection for the individual school an especially difficult one, since the particular needs of the school must be considered.

Many special groups have materials available for school libraries, particularly usable for social studies. As young adults study civil rights and race relations, the pamphlets and audiovisual materials of the Anti-Defamation League of B'nai B'rith are very good. The twelve-volume set of *Life History of the United States*[3] with its accompanying long-playing records is a good addition to the library. *Intercom, a World Affairs Handbook*,[4] is particularly valuable for librarians and teachers, as each of the six yearly issues contains selected, annotated lists of new print and non-print material in world affairs, as well as a special feature section emphasizing one particular area, country, or topic of current interest. An interesting plan for using multi-media for social studies, literature, modern languages, and the sciences has been developed by the Denoyer-Geppert Company. A developmental program for each subject in various grades is worked out. For example, in the study of the geography of the United States in the ninth grade, the objectives of the study are listed, followed by resource materials in the form of specific maps and transparencies, together with "teacher helps"--all available from the Denoyer-Geppert Company.

The whole field of international understanding can be enriched when a teacher sponsors the exchange of personally recorded tapes between his students and those of another country. With 5000 members in seventy countries, the non-profit organization, World Tapes for Education, encourages this program.[5]

An interesting idea of G. P. Putnam's Sons began in 1966 with the production of four portfolios of materials, each pertaining to an historical event in American history, under the general title, The Jackdaws. Each portfolio or kit contains reproductions of documents having to do with the event, as well as maps, charts, engravings, paintings, and costumes of the time. Also included are broadsheets which give modern interpretations and evaluations of the event, together with lists of books to read. A teacher's guide gives suggestions concerning the use of the material, all of which is contained in a sturdy paper case. The first four Jackdaws are: Columbus and the Discovery of America, The Armada, The Mayflower and the Pilgrim Fathers, Magna Carta. Probably they are best used at the senior high school level.

Some teachers of the social studies, especially history teachers, have questioned the extensive use of audiovisual materials, thinking of them only in connection with students who are not capable of understanding written information. Furthermore, they feel that films and recordings may not be historically accurate. Other history teachers believe that good audiovisual aids can capture the atmosphere of an historical moment. It has been said, for example, that "a good recording of Hitler's Nuremberg speeches is almost the only way to give the student some idea of the Fuhrer's captivating and flowery rhetoric."[6] As to the historical accuracy of audiovisual aids, each item, print and non-print, must be criticized individually.

The idea that a single audiovisual medium must be employed if real thought processes are to be developed was tested with an eleventh grade American history class by the Curriculum Development Center of the Carnegie Institute of Technology.[7] The Center used a series of transparencies with the class as the students studied the effect of transportation innovation on the economic growth of five Ohio Valley cities during the first half of the nineteenth century. After showing the first transparency, a discussion between teacher and students followed, until something came up in the discussion which showed the need for the second transparency. It consisted of four overlays that caused the students to think through to the logical conclusion "that improved transportation caused a rise in population because it stimulated economic growth."[8]

Science Department

The needs of the science department for library materials are numerous and widespread. Materials need to be authoritative and up-to-date. When a school offers a variety of courses from basic general science to advanced chemistry, care must be taken to be sure that there are materials containing both simple concepts and detailed, in-depth accounts.

Visual materials and realia have been used with science classes for a long time. These slides, charts, skeletons, etc. are often the property of the science department and are housed and distributed by the department's chairman. However, when library funds are spent on materials for science students, they should be processed and housed by the library. Whether or not they are sent to the science department on long-term loan or circulated to individual science teachers for short periods of time is a matter of need. Regardless of how this is handled, the library's science materials must be available for possible use by other departments or by individual students. Home Economics teachers and members of the physical education department sometimes need materials on subjects such as health and physiology which are usually thought of as subjects in the area of science.

Getting science teachers to see the value of having their students use supplementary library books and magazines can be a real challenge. In a school with traditional scheduling of every course for one period each day, science teachers take time from the lecture-discussion hour for the necessary laboratory work which is a part of most science courses. Thus the explanation for not using library books is "lack of time," or only those references called "identification" books are used occasionally by science students. In the fall, biology students may make a collection of local plants, and they will need such books for identification and descriptive purposes. The broad use of printed materials in science, particularly in the senior high school can be a fine means not only of gaining added knowledge but of creating an interest in the field as a career possibility.

A fine experience for students in any science course and one which can be adapted to meet the needs of students of varying abilities is a study of a variety of science books. The science teachers of East Proviso High School, Maywood, Illinois, and the former librarian, Mrs. Lillian Boula, worked out the following outlines for such a study:

<u>Outline No. 1 - Analysis of a Science Book</u>

I. Book
   A. Title
   B. Author
   C. Publisher
   D. Date

II. Is the book easy to understand?
   If there are illustrations, do they help to understand the main ideas of the book?

III. Presentation
   A. Scholarly
   B. Story-like

IV. Scientific terms
   A. Many
   B. Few
   C. None

V. Scope of book (Table of Contents)

VI. Preface
   A. What did the author expect to accomplish?
   B. Do you think he succeeded?

VII. Index
   A. Complete
   B. Limited

VIII. Glossary
- A. Complete
- B. Limited
- C. Are context explanations adequate?

IX. Read a chapter or a unit.
- A. Informative
- B. Interesting
- C. Indicate coverage (topic)

X. Card Catalog
- A. What did the catalog card tell about the book?
- B. Is there information on this book in any other index in the library? (Book Review Digest)

XI. To which unit or chapter does this book relate?

Outline No. 2 - Biology Book Report

I. Name of book

II. Author

III. Publisher and Date of Publication

IV. Discuss general area covered by book (1 paragraph)
example: Space biology, radiation biology

V. Answer the following questions:
- A. What interesting facts did you discover? List a few.
- B. How do these facts apply to your study of Biology? (Be specific: give examples and illustrations)
- C. Is the author's material reliable? Why?
  1. Author's education and background.
  2. Author's qualifications.
  3. Other books written.

VI. Summary of book
Give a summary of the book in your own words. Limit the summary to no more than a page in length.

Turn in the following on the day the report is written:
1. Outline of report. (Report will be written with the aid of this outline only.)
2. Completed report in ink in regular theme form.

VII. Rules
- A. It's not quantity but quality that counts.

B. Type or write in ink.
C. Use unlined 8 1/2" x 11" paper.
D. One grade point will be subtracted for each day the report is late.

Parts of the outline could be omitted if the teacher feels that it is too detailed for a particular class. In any case, this experience should be limited to one class period of an hour or less. As teacher and library staff work together to assist students as needed, this activity can create a surprising amount of interest in the field.

Science Fair Projects

Student use of library books and magazines as they plan science fair projects is an obvious activity. Some ideas are found in science magazines to which the library regularly subscribes. However, books which contain projects suitable for science fairs must be chosen carefully with considerable help from the science teachers, so that the library has a variety of good resources in adequate numbers readily available. In past years, the school library's materials have been limited in number and kind, so that for this particular need, students have had to go elsewhere. The results of a study of 265 students who entered the state science fair in New Jersey are revealing. In answering the question of where they obtained their reference materials, the largest percentage reported that they obtained their references at home, with the public library being used by twenty-eight percent, and the school library by only eighteen percent.[9] Both the inadequacy of material and its non-availability may be involved here. Some school libraries may have had very strict regulations about borrowing reference books and magazines or they may not have been open at times when the students could use these materials.

Science Fiction

Whether or not science fiction can be considered seriously in connection with the study of science is a controversial subject among teachers. While it is true that some science fiction is very light and fantastic reading, other titles make valuable contributions to the world of science. When well-known science writers, including Ray

Bradbury, Arthur C. Clarke and A. E. Van Vogt, write books of fiction which introduce the popular audience to the world of science, Carefully selected science fiction, for use with high school students, can dramatize the study of science.

Foreign Language Department

Foreign language teaching has expanded in recent years through the incorporation of laboratories using tapes and records for learning the language. A more recent version of the language laboratory is the programmed text-tape course produced for beginning and advanced students of French, German or Spanish.[10] The elementary course in German consists of ten textbooks, twelve tapes, a teacher's manual and a test booklet. The teacher places the appropriate tape on the recorder and stops it as indicated in the textbook. The students use the text to do written work which they check with the answer column in the book, and they make oral responses to be checked with the tape.

Many books consisting of foreign language readers, works of literature and history must be in the school library for the language student. The library should have in its sale paperbacks, a constant supply of good dictionaries in the languages taught in the school. The Traveler's Phrase Book series of paperbacks by Washington Square Press and the Getting Along in French (Spanish, Italian, Russian, German) titles of Bantam Books can be valuable supplementary material which the library can sell. A teacher may want to use as supplementary texts the Bantam dual-language paperbacks containing collections for the literature of Germany, Italy, Spain and others, with the foreign language on one side of the page and its English translation opposite.

Folk tales of the country whose language is being studied are available through a variety of media. But to find such tales in the language itself in a vocabulary and syntax appropriate for beginning and intermediate students' listening comprehension is difficult. For inclusion in the library's collection of microfilm is a well-recommended, original publication entitled _Forty Folk Tales in Spanish: Adaptations and Exercises Designed for Listening Comprehension._[11]

Business Education Department

The business education department may be one in which either teachers or librarians believe that the library can be of little use. It is a fact that a great deal of class time is spent in laboratory work in the major business subjects of typing and shorthand. However, a study of office etiquette and of careers can be incorporated as a part of any business course. Publications for the students of business education are not as numerous as in other areas of the curriculum, and titles in this field are seldom included in basic book selection tools or in the regular reviewing media which librarians have available. The library's collection may be limited largely to pamphlets, magazines and newspapers. The use of the business sections in periodicals such as _Time_, _Business Week_ and _Newsweek_, as well as specific magazines such as _Today's Secretary_ can be well used by business education students.

They can become well acquainted with certain reference books such as Hutchison's _Standard Handbook for Secretaries_ and the _Dictionary of Business and Finance_. The introduction of widely used reference tools as they apply to the secretary or office worker can be valuable to these students. They include books of quotations, etiquette, English dictionaries of various types, atlases and street maps, biographical dictionaries and the _World Almanac_. High schools which have a work-study program administered by the business department should be able to rely on the school library to contain practical material on employer-employee relations. In addition, future secretaries need to know what kind of services public libraries offer to businessmen.

The Arts

Any special programs which the school has must all be given library service to meet their particular requirements. These include: special curriculum for students with low intelligence quotients, work with the visually handicapped, and team teaching. The necessity for good library service is clearly seen in the active part played by the library in a course in Allied Arts taught by a team of teachers at Madison Central-University High School in Madison, Wisconsin.[12]

With the purpose of showing historical relationships in the arts and society, the emphasis is on architecture, music, painting and sculpture, with some study of drama, the dance, literature and history. Maximum use is made of all kinds of audiovisual materials as well as books. Discussions, field trips, and guest lecturers are also used in carrying out this two-semester course. The librarian, Miss Eleanor Bowden, prepared an extensive bibliography for the course. New art filmstrips, books, prints, and music records were added as a part of the regular library acquisitions. The course is taught by a music specialist, an art specialist, and a literature-history teacher. Since the great success of the course at Central-University High School, Larry Everard, the art specialist, has started it in two other Madison schools.

There are a number of ways in which the library directly or indirectly affects all departments of the curriculum. As related to remedial reading programs, the use of multiple texts, "free" reading, book clubs and book discussions, library service is available to any and every teacher.

Remedial Reading

The need for remedial reading programs in the high school has been recognized and put into operation in many systems. All members of the faculty must share responsibility for the reading program, not only the teachers of English, since reading ability affects the learning of every student in every class. A reading specialist can give each teacher assistance in remedial reading in his subject. Librarians must be knowledgeable about what the reading specialist is doing. They need to be aware of special reading demands peculiar to each field. There is a need for many materials of various reading levels for use in the entire curriculum's remedial reading program. The library staff is constantly alert in watching for notices of new publications suitable for this need as they are reviewed in librarians' professional magazines.

Multiple Texts

The use of multiple texts can be a step in the direction of giving students a chance to read more books. Some of these are paperback novels and trade books which do not resemble the traditional textbook in any way. Others may be outlines or guides which are best used as an introduction to a study or as a final review. The Review Texts in Latin, chemistry, world history and other subjects published by AMSCO in paperback form and the Monarch paperbacks are examples of such guides.

Using paperbacks as texts is described by Morris Gall of the Public Schools of Norwalk, Connecticut.[13] The teacher and the class together examine and discuss various possible books of fiction and nonfiction from the many which the teacher brings to the classroom. A number of books may be chosen for supplementary reading, but one is selected to be used as a text. Mr. Gall suggests that the book should be taught as a unit, possibly within one week. With the help of a good study guide, many activities involving small groups and individuals are incorporated in the program.

The Reader's Enrichment Series of Pocket Books, Inc. has both student's and teacher's editions of famous classics and modern novels in paperback form. Both editions contain supplementary material on ideas for writing, vocabulary development, spelling exercises, and suggestions for further reading. These books make good texts.

Paperback Classroom Collections

An interesting experiment in the use of paperbacks for free reading as practiced at Valley High School in Albuquerque, New Mexico, proved to be a good way to have more books easily available through the classrooms of teachers of sophomore English. Paperbacks are purchased from the regular book budget. Although a variety of books is selected, emphasis is on the easy-to-read fiction popular with teenagers. Through the excellent cooperation of the local paperback distributor, many books are examined before final purchase is made. The processing of the books is kept very simple, with only a pocket, book card and date-due slip placed in each book. An average of twenty-five books per class is placed in each sophomore English room; thus the teacher who has three classes receives seventy-five books, the teacher with five classes has 125 books and so on. The books are picked up every six weeks, returned to the library for mending, and immediately replaced with a new collection of different titles. A poster of the simple rules for use is placed in each room. Student librarians in each class handle the routines of keeping track of the books, bringing them to the main library for repair, etc. The responsibility of the teacher is to get acquainted with the books and to do a "selling" job on them. Just how often and in what way these books are made available to the students is up to each teacher. In no case, however, are they used directly for assignments or required reading. Their main purpose is to make easy reading readily available, and they are a supplement to the central library. As it was not possible to have these paperback collections in all English rooms, the sophomores were chosen as they are the first-year students at Valley High School. The thinking here was that these collections would give the students an additional opportunity early in their high school career to continue or to discover the fun of reading. During the eight years of the program's existence it has been used by twenty to thirty English classes each year. As evaluations are made by teachers and students each spring, their enthusiastic response has made it mandatory to continue the program.

Book Clubs

As teachers and librarians sponsor book clubs, reading is encouraged. Social studies teachers may sponsor one of the Challenges Book Clubs, available on the junior and senior level in American history, in citizenship and government, and in world affairs.[14] In each club, students buy a pre-selected group of eight books and receive two bonus books sent to them four times during a school year, at a total cost varying from five dollars to five dollars and sixty cents. The books are well known classics as well as modern titles, carefully chosen to fit into the subject matter. The teacher sponsoring the Club receives special guides for each book with synopses, teaching plans and tests, as well as a free subscription to _Media and Methods_. In addition, twice a year students have an opportunity to buy other books in the field at a discount. Challenges Book Clubs are also available in English and science.

Scholastic Book Services sponsors two book clubs for young people, Teen Age Book Club and Campus Book Club, both of which make books available for thirty to forty cents each. Many of them are original Scholastic titles, while others are reprints. In either case, the books cannot be purchased from regular commercial sources.

Selected paperbacks of various publishers are often sold in the school library. As an individual teacher introduces the study of a particular unit, he asks the librarian to obtain suitable paperbacks in that subject and to make them available for voluntary purchase by his students. A common request of teachers of English when they are studying *Macbeth* is to obtain copies of paperbacks concerning Shakespeare's life and times, and criticism and copies of his writings. The books are sold in the classroom or in the library or both.

Taped Book Discussions

When young people discuss books in class, the discussion can be taped and the tapes put into the library for future use by individual students or by classes. Public libraries sponsor book discussions, too, some of which have been recorded and made available to others. The Detroit Public Library's excellent program of book discussions, moderated by a young adult librarian with teen-age participants, has been taped. Among the tapes produced are discussions of: *The Catcher in the Rye*, *Fail-Safe*, *Letters to a Teen-Age Son*, *Lord of the Flies*, *Slums and Suburbs*, and *Teenagers Ask More Questions*.[15] Listening to taped book discussions gives both teachers and students ideas on the thoughtful reading of books.

Photographing Projects

In many subjects, all sorts of students' projects can be photographed and used for self-evaluation, by classes in other subjects where appropriate, and when the subject is introduced again. As students study the development of the American theatre, for instance, they may make drawings, dioramas, posters, costumes and small stage settings. All can be photographed with a 35 mm camera by the technician-photographer on the library staff. The resulting slides are available as part of the library's collection.

Services Available to All Teachers

What particular services can all teachers, regardless of their subject field, expect from the library?

Obtaining materials on loan is a service which the library provides for all departments. Borrowing material from the state library agency, from other libraries in the region, or from the Library of Congress is a customary service. Sources of material available on free loan from numerous places are known to the library staff. For example, the Bell Telephone System makes available more than fifty films suitable for use with science students, some of them being on the high school level, such as _Memory Devices_ and _Physical Chemistry of Polymers_. The Bell System also has kits for demonstration of conductors and semi-conductors, and for experiments with crystals. They are all described in a brochure obtainable from the local telephone business office.

Notification of New Materials

Another service to all teachers is notification of new library materials. Ideally, as new materials are received, a single catalog card for each item is sent to the appropriate subject teacher. Thus each teacher has a readily available file to which he can refer whenever the need arises. As materials are lost or weeded from the library, teachers are notified to remove the cards for those items. In a school with fifty or more teachers and where the library has only one clerk or typist, this service is more than can be expected. This is particularly true if the cataloging and processing of library materials are done in the local school. As school libraries receive their new materials fully processed and ready for the shelves, and as they buy mechanical duplicating equipment, this service will be more feasible.

Making Bibliographies

The making of bibliographies is a library service which can be expected. As teachers begin a particular study, they often ask for a list of the books, filmstrips, and other materials which the library has on the subject.

As new magazines arrive in the library, the staff takes a

brief look at their contents. Articles relating to the teaching field or to the private interest of particular teachers are noted, and the information sent to them.

Routing Current Journals

The collection of professional materials for faculty and staff is a regular part of the library's contents. In this collection are likely to be certain professional periodicals which are best used when automatically circulated to certain personnel as each new issue arrives. Some are routed to all teachers in a particular department. Others such as the National Education Association's weekly newsletter, Education USA, may be directed only to the principal and his assistants, department chairmen and counselors.

Study of Library Services

Just what services are given by secondary school libraries are shown in the results of a questionnaire given to a group of thirteen schools in a metropolitan New Jersey county and to a nationwide group of thirty-four schools identified by library supervisors as having superior library programs.[16] A checklist of one hundred and ten services all of which fell into the following areas of service was used: reading and reading guidance, supervised study, instruction in library skills, guidance in listening and viewing, social and personal guidance. The same checklist was given by this writer to twenty-seven secondary schools in Albuquerque, New Mexico.

Of the total checklist, the national sample of schools provided the most services - 62.5 percent, while the New Jersey county provided 47.6 percent and the Albuquerque group 39 percent. Eight of the one hundred and ten services were provided in all of the schools in the national sample and the New Jersey county. Although only one service was provided in all of the Albuquerque schools, eight services were provided in all except one school. These services fell into three categories: library instruction, service to faculty and reading guidance, with library instruction being the area in which all schools provided service.

The opinions of twenty-two experts on secondary school library services were obtained when they checked the questionnaire. All of them felt that the following services were of primary importance: (1) orientation to new students and new readers, (2) consultation with faculty on library collections in special subject areas, (3) consultation with faculty on library resources for instructional units, (4) collections of college catalogs available in the library, (5) vocational guidance materials available in the library, (6) orientation of new faculty to library services, (7) orientation of all faculty to new services, (8) interlibrary loan for teachers.[17] As the experts indicated that they considered some services unimportant, several mentioned the need to establish priorities. The inadequacy of the library staff was an explanation given for not checking some items.

Conclusions reached by Gaver and Jones as a result of the study are as follows: (1) the checklist of services has potential as a measure for differentiating among schools with superior, average, or less than average programs of service; (2) the group of school libraries held to have superior programs of service did provide more of the services than the sample group of libraries; (3) services that can be offered with relatively little expense, time and effort on the part of the library staff are offered most frequently in both groups of schools; (4) services that can be offered to groups rather than individuals are offered more frequently; (5) the availability of nonprofessional assistance operates to free professional time for library service to students and teachers; (6) there is a high degree of agreement between the experts and the practicing school librarians in both groups as to which library services are important; (7) the experts are in agreement with school librarians in both groups that expensive and time-consuming activities should be ruled out in favor of the group approach.[18]

The checklist compiled by Gaver and Jones is a good tool for self-study for any secondary school library. It can also serve as a guide to librarians and principals to discover those services which are not being given at all. The relationship between the services and the school's provision of quarters, materials, and particularly library staff is of particular importance as schools attempt to improve library services.

Notes

1. Available from The University of Michigan Audio-Visual

Center, 720 E. Huron, Ann Arbor, Michigan 48104 Nominal service charge.

2. Jerry Weiss and others, The Use of Paperbound Books... National Council of Teachers of English, 508 S. Sixth, Champaign, Illinois. 61820

3. Silver Burdett Co., Park Ave. & Columbus Road, Morristown, N.J. 07960

4. Foreign Policy Association, 345 East 46th, New York. 10017

5. World Tapes for Education, P.O. Box 15703, Dallas, Texas. 75215

6. Walter Ullman, "... Thoughts on the Role of Instructional Media in the Teaching of History," Audiovisual Instruction, XI (December, 1966), 830-831.

7. M. P. Lichtenberg, "New Directions for Obsolete Social Studies Materials," Educational Screen and Audiovisual Guide, XXXV (November, 1966), 20-21.

8. Ibid.

9. Mary V. Gaver, "The Science Collection-New Evidence to Consider," Library Journal, LXXXVI (Feb. 15, 1961), 828-831.

10. Behavioral Research Laboratories, Ladera Professional Center, Box 577, Palo Alto, Calif. 94300

11. University Microfilms, 300 N. Zeeb Rd., Ann Arbor, Michigan. 48106

12. J. L. Everard and Paul Haack, "Allied Arts and the Library," Top of the News, XXII (November, 1965), 104-106.

13. Morris Gall, "Paperbacks and the Social Studies," In Paperbacks in the Schools, edited by Alexander Butman and others. New York: Bantam Books, Inc., 1963.

14. American Education Publications, Inc., Education Center, Columbus, Ohio. 43216

15. Available on loan from Headquarters Library, American Library Association, 50 East Huron, Chicago, Ill. 60611

16. Mary V. Gaver and Milbrey L. Jones, "Secondary Library Services: A Search for Essentials," Teachers College Record, LXVIII (December, 1966), 200-210.

17. Ibid., p. 205.

18. Ibid., p. 207.

Selected Audiovisual Materials

* ALA Conference, 1964, St. Louis. AASL-ASCD-DAVI Pre-conference Institute. Tape. 3 3/4 speed. 2 reels, 60 min. each.
Reel #1 - John Goodlad, Director, University Elementary School, U. of Calif., Los Angeles. Speech-panel discussion: "Emerging Patterns in Curriculum."
Reel #2 - Dr. Harold Drummond, President, NEA Assn. of Supervision and Curriculum Development. Speech: "Effective Curriculum-Joint Enterprise."

* Four Book Talks. Tape. 7.5 speed, 30 min. n.d. Young Adult Dept., Enoch Pratt Free Library, Baltimore, Maryland. 21201

Good examples of four book talks by young adult librarians showing how such talks can vary from one which could be given to a group of non-readers to another on Ethan Frome to more sophisticated young people.

* Midland, Michigan, Senior High School. Book Talks. Tape. 3 3/4 speed, 29 min. n.d.

Round-table discussion by four senior high school students on: One Man's Meat, My Russian Journey, Reveille for a Persian Village. Moderated by an English teacher assisted by two librarians.

New Techniques for Teaching Foreign Languages. 16mm film. sound, black and white, 30 min. 1962. Pierre Capretz, Yale University. Available from Audiovisual Center, Indiana University, Bloomington, Indiana. 47405

Techniques for teaching beginning French, German, Russian, and Spanish to high school students.

* That Dunbar Boy. 16mm film. sound, black and white, 27 min. n.d. Kinescope of one of the Detroit Public Library's "Young America Looks at Books" series.

With the author, John Gould, as guest panelist, a young adult librarian moderates a book discussion by four teenagers.

*"This is a Friendly World" radio interview series. Tape. 21 programs, 15 min. each. n.d.

Portions of radio series by Edwin Randall, dealing with various aspects of India, Japan, and Korea. Include interviews with authors, Asian librarians who have been studying or working in the U.S., and with American librarians who have worked in Asian countries.

* Business Books. Tape. 7.5 speed, 25 min. n.d. Book talk by a young adult librarian from the Detroit Public Library.

Given in high school business and commerical classes.

* Young Adult Librarian Visits an Advanced French Class. Tape. 7.5 speed, 30 min. n.d. Book talk by a young adult librarian from the Detroit Public Library.

Introduces a high school class to a variety of books.

* Available on loan from Headquarters Library, American Library Association, 50 E. Huron, Chicago, Illinois 60611. Round-trip shipping costs are charged. In the case of films, there is also a three-dollar fee.

Selected Readings

The Use of the Library in the Instructional Program

"The Arts, the Humanities, and the School Library," ALA Bulletin, LX (October, 1966), 899-922.

Berner, Elsa. Integrating Library Instruction with Classroom Teaching at Plainview Junior High School. Chicago: American Library Association, 1958.

Butman, Alexander and others, editors. Paperbacks in the Schools. New York: Bantam Books, 1963.

Cohn, Emma. "A Successful Formula for Film Programming," Top of the News, XXI (April, 1965), 247-252.

Compendium of Televised Education. East Lansing, Michigan: Michigan State University, Continuing Education Service, 1965.

Diamond, Robert W. "Instructional Materials within the Seminar," Educational Screen and Audiovisual Guide, XLIV (February, 1965), 32-34.

Dufty, David G. "How I use Records to Teach," Scholastic Teacher, LXXXVIII (April 1, 1966), 5.

Gropper, George L. "Why is a Picture Worth a Thousand Words?" AV Communication Review, XI (July-August, 1963) 75-95.

"How You can Use Television to Strengthen Instruction," School Management, X (May, 1966), 119-123.

Izard, Anne. "Teachers and Librarians Must Come Out of their 'Isolation Booths'," Grade Teacher, LXXXIII (November, 1965), 22.

James, Dan W. "The Teacher and the Library," Education, LXXXVI (May, 1966), 546-549.

Lacy, Grace. "CUE-an Experiment in the Humanities," ALA Bulletin, LX (October, 1966), 918-922.

McCallister, Carlyne. "Teacher Contacts with Library Important," Education, LXXXVI (March, 1966), 408-411.

Mount, Mary. "Librarian and Teacher as a Team," Instructor, LXXV (November, 1965), 71+

Rossoff, Martin. The Library in High School Teaching. 2d ed. New York: The H. W. Wilson Co., 1961.

Schramm, Wilbur. Four Case Studies of Programmed Instruction. New York: Fund for the Advancement of Education, 1964.

Swanson, Viola. "The Librarian--Partner and Teacher," American School Board Journal, CLI (November, 1965), 32-33.

Thomas, R. Murray and Sherwin G. Swartout. Integrated Teaching Materials; How to Choose, Create, and Use Them. rev. and enl. New York: David McKay Co., Inc., 1963.

The Use of the Library in the Teaching of English

Burton, Dwight L. "Literature and the Liberated Spirit," ALA Bulletin, LX (October, 1966), 904-908+

________. Literature Study in the High Schools. New York: Holt, Rinehart and Winston, Inc., 1959.

Norton, Eloise S. "Authors on Tape," School Libraries, XV (March, 1966), 35-37.

Sheridan, Marion C. and others. The Motion Picture and the Teaching of English. New York: Appleton-Century-Crofts, 1965.

Valdivia, Fernando J. "The Bard with the Bell and Howell," Audiovisual Instruction, XII (January, 1967), 41-44.

The Use of the Library in the Teaching of Social Studies

Brown, Ralph A. "The Use of Paperbacks in High School Social Studies Classes," School Libraries, XI (May, 1962), 16-20.

Collings, Dorothy, "Improving the Teaching of World Affairs," School Libraries, XV (October, 1965), 28-34.

Fraser, Dorothy M. "Annual Review of Curriculum Materials," Social Education, XXIX (April, 1965), 228-237.

Gall, M. "Using Paperback Classics in the Social Studies," Social Education, XXVII (March, 1963), 141-144.

Gritzner, Charles F. and Philip B. Larimore. "Educational Media Available to the Teacher of Geography," Social Education, XXX (December, 1966), 620-623.

Trump, J. Lloyd. "Focus on Change: Organizing for Teaching the Social Studies," Social Education, XXX (March, 1967), 163-167.

The Use of the Library in the Teaching of Science

Boula, Lillian. "The Library and the Science Department," Illinois Libraries, XLIII (January, 1961), 51-54.

Vedro, Alfred S. "Shades of Jules Verne and H. G. Wells," School Paperback Journal, I (February, 1965), 18-19.

West, Marcia. "Communication in Science Teaching," School Paperback Journal, I (February, 1965), 7-9.

The Use of the Library in the Teaching of Business Education, Art, and Foreign Languages

Jassy, William. "The Modern Language Revolution Needs a Coordinated Paperback Program," School Paperback Journal, II (December, 1965), 20-22.

Peters, Frances E. "It Must be Somewhere! Library Service to Secretarial Students," Top of the News, XXII (June, 1966), 403-407.

Putney, Agnes B. "Teaching Shorthand with the Help of an Overhead Projector," Educational Screen and Audiovisual Guide, XLIV (February, 1965), 34-35.

Sloan, William J. "Art Films for Young Adults," Top of the News, XXII (November, 1965), 48-52.

The Use of the Library in the Reading Program

Gaver, Mary V. "What Research Says about the Teaching of Reading and the Library," The Reading Teacher, XVII (December, 1963), 184-191.

Karlin, Robert. Teaching Reading in High School. Indianapolis, Indiana: Bobbs-Merrill Co., Inc., 1964.

Reading Instruction in Secondary Schools. (Perspectives in Reading No. 2) Newark, Delaware: International Reading Association, 1964.

Ticknor, William E. "Education toward Maturity," Top of the News, XX (May, 1964), 269-272.

Veatch, Jeannette. How to Teach Reading with Children's Books. New York: Bureau of Publications, Teachers College, Columbia University, 1964. (pamphlet)

Chapter V

Reference Service

The reference function of the school library is a part of the total guidance service. Reference can be described as the process of locating information; such help must be given to many of the library's users. Even when there exists a good program of training for teachers and students, the day by day inquiries require reference service of all kinds. This may include assistance in the choice of books and other materials, a problem with the use of the card catalog, guidance in using encyclopedia indexes, and finding answers to specific questions through the use of reference books.

The Reference Collection

A good collection of reference books is fundamental to good reference service, as many of the inquiries are for specific information. These books which are so organized as to make specific information readily accessible make up a separate collection in most libraries. The careful selection of these reference books is an important task of school librarians. Since they are usually more expensive than regular trade books, special care must be taken to purchase those titles which really will be used. They must be related closely to the subjects in the school's curriculum. In selecting reference books, Lowrie recommends that the following points be considered in evaluating each title:

1. Format--size, print, illustrations, paper, and so on.
2. Age appeal--vocabulary, appropriate style, content.
3. Arrangement of material--alphabetical or subject, cross references, index or fact guides.
4. Authority--up-to-dateness, objectivity.
5. Cost--appropriate to use.
6. Balance--in relation to the total collection.[1]

Encyclopedias, dictionaries, handbooks, and other specialized books make up the reference collection. "Encyclopedias that are authoritative, reasonably new, and suitable in appearance and content are the backbone of any school library's reference collection," says Rossoff.[2] There is a need for some which are written in simple language, such as Compton's Pictured Encyclopedia and the World Book Encyclopedia; other so-called "adult" encyclopedias such as the Encyclopaedia Britannica and the Encyclopedia Americana must be available. Since they contain all kinds of information, they are often the starting place in a search for specific facts, as well as their obvious use for an over-all view of a subject. Their pictures, diagrams, maps and charts may be available only in one particular encyclopedia and in no other books in a library. Among the valuable encyclopedias in subject areas are the Encyclopedia of Science and Technology and the Encyclopedia of World Art (both McGraw-Hill publications), the Dictionary of American History, the Encyclopedia of Sports, and the Encyclopedia of Child Care.

Both abridged and unabridged English language dictionaries are necessary, as are ones used for studying foreign languages. Evaluations of the various language dictionaries available should be carefully studied and the books themselves examined before purchase is made.

Reference books in special subjects are necessary to have, such as the Harvard Dictionary of Music and the Poetry Handbook. Numerous biographical dictionaries are a necessity, as they are useful in many subjects taught in high schools. Care must be taken to have a variety of kinds: those containing biographies of people of one country, those limited to one period of time, those of one occupation, ones of an all-inclusive nature. As students become acquainted with biographical dictionaries, it is important that they learn to distinguish between certain titles. One of the most common mistakes that high school students make is to ask for Who's Who when they want Who's Who in America. It is valuable that they know that Webster's Biographical Dictionary includes brief biographies and pronunciations of names of people of all times and countries, both living and dead. That biographical information can be found in encyclopedias must be emphasized, and the value of the Index volume of the Encyclopaedia Britannica for simple identification of people should be pointed out.

Having current and up-to-date material is a necessity which can be answered by having reference books that are frequently revised or which appear annually. Since the expense of frequent revision of all articles in an encyclopedia makes this prohibitive, the customary practice is to do partial revision constantly. In order to update all material, a publisher may produce annual volumes, such as the Yearbook of the Encyclopedia of Science and Technology and the Encyclopedia Americana's Yearbook, thus allowing the library staff to fill requests for current information. The annual publication of the World Alamanac and the U. S. Government Organization Manual are necessary acquisitions for current information. Current and recent information found in magazines makes the Reader's Guide to Periodical Literature or its abridged edition a mandatory purchase.

Selection

Selected lists of recommended reference books for the secondary school library are located in the ALA's Basic Book Collection for Junior High Schools and a Basic Book Collection for High Schools. For reviews of selected new reference books of all kinds, Frances Neel Cheney's "Current Reference Books" appearing in each issue of the Wilson Library Bulletin is excellent. The semi-monthly Booklist and Subscription Books Bulletin contains lengthy reviews of one or two reference titles. School Library Journal includes reference books in its listings of many new publications. As titles become obsolete or are found to be of little value, they should be removed from the shelves, so that the reference collection will remain largely a working one.

In addition to books, the reference collection is likely to include single maps, pictures, and a limited number of audiovisual materials. Two good sources of maps are the United States Government and the National Geographic Society, while pictures are available from museums and societies. Of course, both can be purchased from commercial firms.

Location

Should reference books be on open shelves accessible to all, or should they be in a closed area available only to the library staff; or should they be shelved by subject along with the non-fiction trade books? People who advocate that reference books be placed on open shelves do so because of their belief that all library materials should be easily accessible. Those who believe in closed shelves for the reference collection see no value in browsing in reference books. They also see the problem of a particular reference title not being quickly available. Reference volumes disappear or have pages removed more easily when they are on open shelves. When reference books are shelved with the corresponding non-fiction titles, all books which the library has are together by subject; but having to go to widely scattered areas on the shelves to get at a particular reference book is a great inconvenience for librarians as well as students and teachers. Probably the best arrangement is to have most reference books in a closed area with duplicate copies of certain frequently used titles on open shelves separate from the trade books. Maps and pictures require special filing cabinets which should be located in the reference area.

Other Sources for Answers to Reference Questions

Some trade books, particularly those with good indexes, are useful for finding answers to reference problems. As subjects are looked up in the card catalog, one is frequently referred to trade books. However, students who are doing research often need a librarian's help as they look for subjects in the card catalog. No matter how well students are able to use the *Reader's Guide*, reference books, or to locate particular titles and authors through the card catalog, they have great difficulty in understanding the subject approach to the catalog. That subjects can be looked up under different wordings or under key words must be taught. Students also need to learn to imagine all the various ways in which a subject could be listed and then check the catalog until the proper term is discovered. Some of the entries in Sears *List of Subject Headings* sound very peculiar to young people. For example, "plurality of worlds" is hardly a subject that a teen-ager would think of. Placing a copy of *Sears* near the card catalog helps to familiarize the library user with the wording of subjects and with the way many subjects are organized. But in any case, the library staff must be alert to the needs of the student and the teacher who appear to be having difficulty using the card catalog.

Techniques

As members of the library staff function as reference librarians they need to acquire certain methods and techniques. Some simple requests for information can be quickly and easily answered when a librarian immediately can pinpoint the subject into which the question falls and when he knows his reference collection well. Other questions necessitate a good deal of thought and investigation in various sources. It is often necessary to make inquiries of the student regarding the precise nature of his request, the quantity of information desired, the depth to which he wants to study the subject, and the details of his teacher's requirements. The experienced librarian relies greatly on her memory, particularly as the same or similar requests keep appearing year after year; but it is unwise to be so inflexible as to refer automatically only to sources previously used, and to neglect newly acquired reference sources.

Observing clues in one reference which lead to additional information is important. In working with students the pressure of time sometimes gets in the way of doing a thorough job of giving reference service. Knowing that the student has a limited amount of time to spend in the library also affects the nature of the material you obtain for him. This brings up the perennial question of how much time a librarian should spend on digging out information for students, and to what extent she should do the actual work of locating information. The answer depends on certain factors. If the students have had thorough and recent training in how to find information, particularly if it was in a field in which they are now seeking help, they should be reminded of a few points previously learned, and allowed to go ahead on their own. In the case of a student who has little background in library usage and who may not be capable of grasping more than the simplest things, every help must be given to carry him as far as he can go in gaining a successful library experience. For the student who is capable of going into considerable depth in his investigation, the librarian must be willing and able to lead him even beyond the confines of the school library, by borrowing materials from other sources or suggesting other community resources for the student to follow up. Judgement on the part of the librarian enters into decisions of this kind, as it does in relation to every reference request. But since the school library is part of an educational institution, the library staff needs constantly to keep in mind that learning to become independent users of a library is a major goal of its program.

Self-help

In encouraging self-help on the part of students and teachers, the library staff prepares bibliographies of reference works in particular subjects for distribution as needed. Labels, signs, and posters giving locations and listings of reference materials are made. When unabridged dictionaries, atlases, Reader's Guides, and other volumes are on special stands and tables, these are easy to point out to library users.

Record-keeping

The library staff can help to meet future reference requests by keeping records of where the answers to certain difficult questions can be found. Nothing is quite as irritating and time-consuming as trying to remember just where certain information was found for a request known to have been filled on a previous occasion. A card file of these questions listed by appropriate subjects can be of great assistance, but there is the danger of neglecting to check new acquisitions which may contain better material. Making indexes of material, provided they are not duplicates of ones already in existence, can be helpful. The same can be said for bibliographies. Consideration of future needs in connection with making of indexes and bibliographies must be carefully thought out before this time-consuming work is done. In the field of state and local government, indexes and bibliographies may fill a real need.

Whether or not to keep records of reference services is a serious question in the administration of the school library. Although public libraries have done so for many years, no published research is available on what is done in this area by school libraries. This could be a valuable practice for school librarians either on a regular daily basis or a "spot check" during one or two months of the year. Evaluating the effectiveness of reference work is difficult if not impossible, but certain other records are easy to keep. Comparing the total amount of time spent on reference work with the other parts of the total library program could be useful. A study of the nature of the questions could reveal where additional materials were needed or reference tools in a new area were required. Reference records could also be helpful in planning the program of teaching library usage. Rothstein sees the trends in the measurement and evaluation of reference service, particularly in public libraries, as falling into two groups: (1) Enumeration of reference questions, (2) reference questions classified by type, subject, purpose or effect.[3] He suggests that the former really doesn't mean much and is likely to be incomplete, but that the total number in itself may be impressive. The second group includes separate listing by Dewey classes, by the purpose served, by the kind of material used (reference, regular shelves, card catalog, pamphlets), by effect (percentage of questions answered). Such records have possibilities for effective use by school librarians.

Even though no reference statistics are regularly kept, the listing of reference questions from time to time can be of interest to faculty, administrators and students. Unusual questions asked and answered make good publicity and can be a regular feature of the section on library news of the school's newspaper. For the library staff, such a list can give a sense of accomplishment.

Here follows a partial list of reference questions asked at a senior high school where the writer was the librarian for twelve years.

Frequent requests:

1. Information on these "perennial" topics (requested largely by tenth graders): voting by 18-year-olds, juvenile delinquency, teen-age marriage, capital punishment, narcotics.

   "Perennials" requested by more sophisticated students: unidentified flying objects, adult-teenager relationships, extra-sensory perception, individual freedoms.

2. Curriculum related topics: the circulation system of humans and animals, identification of plants, current events, disease, vocabulary study, child care, various kinds of maps work in most geography and history classes, quotations, biographical information particularly in literature and history courses.

Specific questions:

1. What is a good book of fiction with a school teacher as the main character?
2. Picture of William Shakespeare as a child
3. Where can I find some plans for building furniture?
4. Pictures of various breeds of cattle
5. Who was Poet Laureate of England in 1912?
6. What is the average lifetime of a collie?
7. What scholarships are available at Stephens College?
8. How is nylon fabric made?
9. When did John Donne live?
10. How high is the tallest peak in the Rocky Mountains?
11. Who were the Southern generals in the Civil War?
12. Who was prime minister of Canada in 1941?
13. When was printing invented?
14. Where is the largest gold mine in the world?
15. When was the opera _Madame Butterfly_ written?
16. What paperbacks on psychology are available for less than a dollar?

Good reference service, quickly and accurately given, elicits much admiration and respect for the library staff. It can be at the very heart of the library program. The administration of the reference aspect of the school library calls for careful consideration, planning, and evaluation of the reference collection and its proper use.

Notes

1. Jean E. Lowrie, "What Goes on the Reference Shelf of the Library," Instructor, LXXIII (November, 1963), 53-55.

2. Martin Rossoff, _The Library in High School Teaching_, 2nd ed., The H. W. Wilson Co., 1961, p. 137.

3. Samuel Rothstein, "The Measurement and Evaluation of Reference Service," _Library Trends_, XII (January, 1964), 456-472.

Selected Audiovisual Materials

Young Adult Librarian Discusses Reference Aids. Tape. 7.5 speed. 30 min. Moderator: Marcia Keller, Young Adult Librarian, Detroit Public Library

Excellent presentation of reference books to a high school class.

Selected Readings

Darling, Richard L. "Selection and Reference Use in the School Library," [government publications] Library Trends, XV (July, 1966), 87-92.

Galvin, Thomas J. "Building a Strong Reference Collection," Choice, III (June, 1966), 279-282.

Hutchins, Margaret. Introduction to Reference Work. Chicago: American Library Association, 1944.

In spite of its publication date, this book has many ideas on the scope, selection, organization, and administration of reference service which are helpful to the modern school librarian.

Marantz, Sylvia. "Maps in the Library," School Libraries, XVI (Winter, 1967), 25-28.

Rowland, Arthur Ray. Reference Services. Camden, Connecticut: Shoe String Press, 1964.

Tripp, Edward. "On Library Panic," Library Journal, XC (October 15, 1965), 4514-4516.

Needs of students preparing for college to learn basic research skills and to be familiar with a variety of reference books.

Chapter VI

Selection and Acquisition of Materials

Selection Principles and Policies

As the library's role in the total instructional program grows in significance, the selection of materials to support its part of the total program becomes more and more challenging to the library staff. In an effort to enunciate principles of selection, the American Library Association, individual school systems across the country, the faculty of many alert and progressive schools, as well as several professional librarians' associations have, from time to time, made statements relative to the selection of material. Certainly underlying an understanding of the selection process must be an acceptance of the principles laid down in the School Library Bill of Rights.

> ...The American Association of School Libraries reaffirms the Library Bill of Rights of the American Library Association and asserts that the responsibility of the school library is:
>
> To provide materials that will enrich and support the curriculum, taking into consideration the varied interests, abilities, and maturity levels of the pupils served.
>
> To provide materials that will stimulate growth in factual knowledge, literary appreciation, aesthetic values, and ethical standards.
>
> To provide a background of information which will enable pupils to make intelligent judgements in their daily life.
>
> To provide materials on opposing sides of controversial issues so that young citizens may develop under guidance the practice of critical reading and thinking.
>
> To provide materials representative of the many religious, ethnic, and cultural groups and their contributions to our American heritage.
>
> To place principle above personal opinion and reason

above prejudice in the selection of materials of the highest quality in order to assure a comprehensive collection appropriate for the users of the library.

A good guide to writing a selection policy is contained in the statement, "Policies and Procedures for Selection of School Library Materials," approved in 1961 by the Board of Directors of the American Association of School Librarians.[1] It suggests the following contents for such a policy statement:

1) A statement of the philosophy of book selection for school libraries such as is given in the School Library Bill of Rights of the American Association of School Librarians, or the Book Selection Policy (tentative) of the School Library Association of California, Northern Section.

2) A statement that the Governing Board of the district is legally responsible for the selection of library materials.

3) A statement detailing the delegation of this responsibility to professionally trained personnel.

4) An outline of the procedures and criteria to be applied throughout the school or district in selecting library materials.

5) A routine procedure for handling library materials that may be questioned by individuals or groups within the community.

In addition to such general principles, there is usually included in the educational goals of the total instructional program of an individual school system a statement which indicates competence in reading, listening, and observing as specific goals. To further clarify the necessity for careful selection of materials, some school systems have adopted their own statement of selection policy which encompasses both print and audiovisual media. Such written statements serve as a basis for common agreement among those who are responsible for selection and a clear and detailed guide to their responsibilities. The statement is often a result of faculty discussion on such topics as the student's right to read and freedom of inquiry. In planning such a discussion a careful study of the statement of the National Council of Teachers of English entitled The Students' Right to Read is invaluable.[2]

The school systems which have handbooks for librarians include criteria for selection. In the Librarian's Handbook published by authority of the Board of Directors of Shoreline School District No. 412 of Seattle, Washington, there are two selection criteria statements, one for books and the other for audiovisual materials. The one for books lists criteria under the following headings: suitability of materials for various types of use, qualifications of the subject matter of the book, format of the book, recognized value. Its statement of the criteria for selecting audiovisual materials is as follows:

> Content should effectively fulfill the desired objectives of the teacher and the curriculum.
>
> Content should be true to fact or true to life and true to text if based on writing.
>
> Preaching, condescension, loaded words, cheapness, or coy humor should be avoided.
>
> Photography is an art. Therefore, in addition to the above criteria, judge filmstrips, slides and other visual materials for their style, imagination of presentation, originality and other aesthetic qualities.[3]

How Materials are Chosen

It is very easy to limit one's selection to the printed materials that one actually sees: new books and magazines on the shelves of the local public library or book store, in the exhibits of various media at conventions, those shown by publishers' representatives who come to the library. This is the expedient thing to do. Although new materials are often appealing in themselves, their newness is not the only factor to be taken into account when making selections. A library which contains only new and recent materials will miss many of the books which time has proved to be of great value.

Ideally all materials, both print and audiovisual, are actually read or examined before a decision is reached to purchase them or not. Both books and audiovisual materials can be borrowed and examined by individuals and groups. Some large school districts arrange to have new materials of all kinds available in a central place for examination and previewing. Others twice a year obtain the collections, Books on Exhibit[4] and the Combined Paperback Exhibit,[5] for examination by school personnel. These are valuable aids in the selection process.

Book Selection Guides

However, in the daily task of selection, librarians rely greatly on many kinds of lists and catalogs containing materials, both print and audiovisual, selected and annotated by experts.[6] The best lists and catalogs for choosing books are those compiled by people--often librarians and subject specialists--who have read critically the books listed. The review or annotation gives an idea of the subject matter, for what level it is written (both as to comprehension and interest), the format and complete bibliographical data. Before relying upon a selection tool, one must evaluate the reliability of the individual or the organization which produced it. Also to be considered is its recentness since old lists usually contain titles no longer in print or which have had more recent editions. Published lists vary from those recommended for a new library's basic collection, such as the Junior High School Catalog published in 1965 containing 3278 titles, to the many shorter lists designed to meet particular needs, such as Reading Ladders for Human Relations and Key to the Past. The selected lists compiled by public libraries from books in their collections which they recommend for young people are often good sources of selection for the school library. The Enoch Pratt Free Library of Baltimore produces numerous such lists, and the annual publication of the New York Public Library, Books for the Teen Age, is a valuable one. Current professional periodicals devoted exclusively or largely to reviewing new books and other media are required reading for the librarian and his staff. In a study of book selection aids used by twenty-one junior college libraries in California, the three magazines most frequently used were: Library Journal, Choice, and Booklist and Subscription Books Bulletin.[7] When schools are required to limit their purchases to specific materials on lists issued by their state departments of education, a form of censorship is being imposed. Rather the state authorities should urge school libraries to select titles from lists published by certain organizations recognized as being authoritative, reliable and knowledgeable, such as the American Library Association and its various divisions, the various departments of the National Education Association, the National Science Foundation, and the International Reading Association.

Selection of Magazines

To meet needs for information on recent happenings the library must contain magazines, newspapers and pamphlets. Today's high school student needs up-to-date information about happenings in many subjects, from the usual current events in social studies classes to art exhibits and last month's trip to outer space. Recent information to fill requests on topics not related to classroom assignments but of a personal interest must be available. For easy access to information available in recent periodicals, all high school libraries should subscribe to the semi-monthly index, Reader's Guide to Periodical Literature. For small high schools, the abridged edition of the Guide indexing forty-one magazines may be adequate. The library must subscribe to all of the magazines indexed therein if maximum use is to be made of it. If all Reader's Guide magazines are not available, the library staff constantly runs the risk of being unable to supply material referred to in the Reader's Guide and thus disappointing the student who has found reference to information for which there is likely to be no substitute. In addition, other magazines meeting both the curricular and the personal needs of the student are necessary. A school which has courses in auto-mechanics will need additional magazines in that field. Young people in some areas will be enthusiastic about hunting, so that the library will need additional magazines to meet that interest. The school which has an active foreign language club will want to subscribe to special magazines not indexed in the Reader's Guide. To get an idea of the thousands of magazines which can be subscribed to, the librarian should see the latest edition of Ulrich's International Periodicals Directory and its supplements.[8] For reviews of new periodicals, the librarian is referred to the Library Journal, which contains such reviews as a regular feature.

Selection of Pamphlets

Pamphlets are another source of recent information. Since

they are sometimes written to favor one point of view, the selector needs to watch to see that the information is factual and unbiased. As much pamphlet material is free, it is easy to yield to the temptation of automatically acquiring it for the library. The *Vertical File Index* is a good guide to selected free and inexpensive material, which is usually four to eighty pages in length and unbound. The regular reading of professional magazines will reveal other new pamphlets. The library may want to have a regular subscription to certain pamphlets, such as the *Foreign Policy Bulletin*.

Selection of Audiovisual Material

What tools are used for the selection of audiovisual and other non-print media?[9] An invaluable book which describes the various catalogs generally available is *Guides to Newer Educational Media: Films, Filmstrips, Phono-records, Radio, Slides, Television*, by Margaret I. Rufsvold and Carolyn Guss. The guides one wants to buy or subscribe to can be chosen from this book. For each catalog listed, complete bibliographical information is given, in addition to information on the catalog's scope, arrangement, entries and special features. There are reviews of new catalogs as a regular feature of the magazine *Educational Screen and A-V Guide*. For a complete listing of all audiovisual titles available as of 1964 the fourteen-volume *Educational Media Index* is available. A valuable monthly service reviewing recordings of spoken words, suitable for schools, is *Audio Cardalog*.[10] By putting the reviews on three by five inch punched cards for the title, author and subject of each recording, the reviews can be loaned easily to more than one person for possible selection and then can be filed in the library for future reference. Each card includes: synopsis, rating and appraisal, utilization, record label.

The *EFLA Evaluations* of the Educational Film Library Association are a good source of reviews for educational films.[11] They also appear on cards.

Certain magazines often read by school personnel are initiating or expanding their reviews of audiovisual media. For example, Scholastic Teacher began a new section with its October 7, 1966 issue entitled "New Educational Materials" for which a panel of classroom teachers and administrators preview a sampling of new records, tapes, filmstrips, study prints and transparencies. Whenever possible, the panel members also actually use the new materials with students so that they can make more realistic evaluations as to their use. The librarian needs to be aware that reviews of both books and audiovisual aids are found also in Atlantic Monthly, Consumer Bulletin, English Journal, Instructor, PTA Magazine, Science, and other readily available magazines.

Other sources of selected buying lists sometimes missed because they are not advertised to the extent of those of regular commercial producers are professional organizations such as the National Education Association, the National Association of Radio and Television Broadcasters, and the Association of Childhood International. Such groups as federal and state departments, Unesco, and the U. S. Chamber of Commerce are additional sources of selection lists. Colleges and schools often list their monthly acquisitions, or make lists for specific local needs. These also can be considered sources for selection by the local school. The best lists, taking into consideration their source, contain critical reviews or annotations by people who have read or examined the items. A real service is contributed by the classroom teacher who makes a note evaluating a film, a record, or a book after he has used it with his students. Whether a teacher finds library material to be of use to meet the particular needs of his students is the real test of its value. Consequently, when an on-the-job evaluation is made using such a form as the one below, it can be made available to others.

Evaluation Form

Circle whichever applies:	Date of evaluation__________
Book 16mm film 8mm film	Fill in whichever applies:
	Length______________
Disc recording Tape recording	No. of frames________
	Size________________
Filmstrip Slides	
Other_______________	Subject matter______________

Cost, rental fee ____________

Title ____

Author (if any) ______________________________________

Publisher or producer _________________________________

Summary ____

(Continue on back) ___________________________________

Format (Rate as excellent, good, fair, poor):

Binding ________________ Print ________________

Sound ________________ Photography ____________

Additional criticisms __________________________________

If recommended, for what level or need? _________________

____

(Permission to copy the above is freely given)

Selection of Audiovisual Equipment

In addition to selecting the films, filmstrips, slides and recordings themselves, the library staff and the faculty choose the equipment necessary for their use. Since there are numerous companies advertising audiovisual equipment, it is easy simply to select the ones most attractively advertised or which are for sale locally. But again the wise procedure is to examine and read descriptions of various ones, using selection criteria such as: performance, sturdiness, reputation, safety, how it operates, provisions for service and repair. In addition, special criteria for projectors, record players, teaching machines, slide projectors, television receivers and other items are necessary. Certain questions must be considered. Is it simple to thread this tape recorder? Is the focusing of this projector easy? Does this record player reproduce records of various speeds? Of great help to the local library staff are the new equipment evaluations made by the Technological Development Project of the National Education Association and the Library Technology Program of the American Library Association. In addition, manuals such as the A-V Instructional Materials Manual written by James W. Brown and Richard B. Lewis often include descriptions of equipment.[12]

Using Publishers' Catalogs

Nothing has been said about using publishers' and producers' catalogs as selection aids. As numerous catalogs arrive daily in the library mail, they appear to be obvious sources for selection. With more and more money available from local, state and federal sources, there is a temptation simply to order a thousand dollars worth of unspecified materials from a good salesman, or a publisher's catalog which says, "These books are suitable for purchase by the school library with Title II funds." Thus the salesman or the publisher becomes the selector of materials for your library! Actually, exclusive reliance on catalogs of publishers and producers is a dangerous practice. Since they are commercial outlets, they describe their products in the best possible light in order to sell them. As time goes on, however, the experienced librarian discovers that particular publishers and producers can be relied on to have available good materials, well written and produced. The visit of the sales representatives for these companies is an opportunity to examine new materials and note certain items for possible purchase.

A perfect job of selection is impossible, and every librarian has a few books or filmstrips that she wishes had never been purchased. But the use of expertly compiled lists and guides, together with slow and careful consideration of each possible title in relation to the needs of the individual school, will go a long way toward making wise selections.

Professional Collection

Although most of the library's collection is intended for student use, the local school also should have professional materials for the use of teachers and administrators. However, school personnel will doubtless receive certain periodicals as members of professional organizations, and there is also likely to be a library of materials for their use at the central office of the school system. In addition, public and college libraries in the community will have materials on the subject of education. But having information conveniently available in the local school is a service which should be provided by the library. Simply in order for teachers to keep up with new developments in such fields as curriculum, school buildings, guidance services, and methods of teaching, the school library serves its faculty and administrators. When teachers take courses toward advanced degrees, the local school's professional collection can supplement the college and public library's collection. In addition, the professional journals, pamphlets, books, and audiovisual materials are useful when teachers prepare reports for school committees.

In order to assure high quality of professional materials, the same selection criteria as used for materials for student use should be applied. The publication, The Teachers' Library, is a good tool for the selection of these materials.[13] Saturday Review in its monthly education issue includes reviews of new books. Many professional education magazines contain reviews of print and non-print media in special subject areas. The annual listing of selected books in the May issue of the NEA Journal and the section, "Books for Educators," in School and Society are good selection guides. The professional collection should be an important part of the library.

Paperbacks

Something must be said on the subject of paperbacks. This subject has been discussed by school librarians for the past decade. Although there is still occasional reference to paperbacks as ephemeral and unworthy of being on library shelves, gone are the days when paperbacks intended only for light reading--often called "trash" by librarians--were published. The role of the paperback has been recognized by the establishment of the Paperback Book Information Library at Teachers College, Columbia University. Its two-fold purpose is: (1) to disseminate information on the "Paperback Revolution," (2) to encourage research on this emerging medium of instruction. In addition, a conference on "Design for Paperbacks" held at Columbia University in June 1966, provided a means for publishers and librarians to discuss problems.

The number of paperbacks has increased greatly, from 2615 in 1961 to 9317 in 1965, with many of the titles being reprints of well-known books and others being original titles, all possible additions for the high school library. Publishers have taken into consideration suggestions for improving cover and format and for materials to be published. The monthly publication of Paperbound Books in Print, the annual Paperback Goes to School, and the magazine

Media and Methods (formerly School Paperback Journal) are of great service in the selection of paperbacks. Whether or not to have paperbacks in the school library is no longer a question, as they have proved their worth. The attractiveness to young people of the paperback, even when the title is also available in a hardback edition, is very noticeable. The initial cost of paperbacks is comparatively low. Paperback editions are the only ones available of some badly needed books. The availability of special treatment to the bindings such as that done by Vinabind of St. Louis and Hertzberg-New Method, Inc., of Jacksonville, Illinois, at low cost, adds to their length of use. Books which have long been out of print are being published in paperback form. Libraries which sell paperbacks have found it to be a greatly appreciated part of their regular service. Certain decisions, however, need to be made. Should paperbacks be bought as additional copies of a popular book? Are paperbacks a wise choice for areas in which the library needs materials but in which only a little use is expected? The whole question of processing paperbacks is to be taken into consideration. But there should be no question about their usability in today's high school library.

There are two particular areas in which selection for high school reading is limited: books for the remedial reader and books for the teenager who can read but does only the minimum required by his teachers. To meet the needs of the former for books with simple vocabulary but on the interest level of teenagers, a few publishers have made particular efforts. For the young adult who does not like to read, the library staff will find the guide Fare for the Reluctant Reader very useful, as well as lists compiled by teachers who have found particular titles especially successful.

Basic Considerations in Selection

The wealth of books, films, filmstrips, tapes, pictures, and other media available is in itself a challenge to those responsible for selecting school library materials. The needs of the local school must be the chief factor. There are, however, certain so-called "basic" books which nearly every high school needs, regardless of its size or its educational goals, such as particular reference books and literary classics. But for the rest of the collection, right from the establishment of a new school, the library staff as well as other administrators must gain as much background as possible about the community where the school is located. What are the community's mores? How do the families earn their living? What are the goals of the parents for their children? In addition, the library staff consults with administrators and teachers to become very familiar with curriculum plans. What proportion of the student body is enrolled in the college preparatory curriculum? Will there be a remedial reading program? What foreign languages are taught? What courses are taught without textbooks? These and many other considerations directly affect the choice of materials for the library's collection.

As the selection of library materials continues, there will be opportunities to find out more closely the needs and interests of teachers and students. Changes may take place in the curriculum which will necessitate development of the library's collection in new directions. Problems will constantly arise, however, making decisions of selection a difficult job even for knowledgeable and intelligent people. Whether to purchase books or audiovisual material to meet a specific need can be a real problem. The learning which takes place by the use of a good filmstrip in a biology class, for example, by a teenager with limited cultural background and who has been in remedial reading classes in his elementary school years can be considerable. One of the advantages of books is that they do not require a machine for their use, and consequently can be used anywhere. However, as technology develops small projectors and recorders, more and more libraries have them to loan along with films and recordings. There is a certain appeal of the pictorial over the printed. Perhaps this is simply the appeal of something different. If this is the case, it is a real clue to the selector of library materials: there must be a variety of kinds of media, all easily available for individual and group use. But along with a variety of media comes the best in books, tapes, etc., for use of one particular school, with each item considered on its individual merits.

Problem Areas and Censorship

There are certain areas of knowledge sometimes considered controversial which librarians have found to be real problems for selection, particularly for materials for libraries connected with public schools where young minds are being formed. These areas are: economics, politics, race, religion, sex, and certain works of literature. Selection in these subjects can most easily result in censorship, as the line between the two can be very thin. Censorship may be practiced by the librarian in the name of selection. What is described as a "balanced collection" may be simply the acquisition of "the materials that the teachers want," to the exclusion of materials in areas of the curriculum in which teachers never make recommendations, and with no thought to the personal interests of students. The librarian may choose not to buy a particular book because it is "controversial," "doesn't meet the needs of our curriculum," "doesn't fit in with our community interests," is "too difficult for our students to read"--all in the name of selection. Actually these may be acts of negative censorship. A surprising number of school and public librarians practice this kind of censorship, according to Marjorie Fiske's study in California.[14] Of the 204 librarians interviewed, 18 percent habitually avoided and another 41 percent sometimes avoided any material which "is known to be controversial or which they believe might become controversial." As librarians and other members of their institutions discovered controversial materials already in their libraries, some form of restriction was placed on their use in 82 percent of the cases.

In addition to this self-imposed censorship by librarians, there exists pressure from well-meaning groups such as the American Legion, the Citizens for Decent Literature, the D.A.R., and the Minute Women of the U.S. to avoid purchasing certain books or to remove others from the shelves. The simple existence of these vocal groups and their reputation for censorship causes a climate of fear to exist. The reading of issues of the _Newsletter on Intellectual Freedom_ reveals numerous cases where organizations forced certain books to be withdrawn from libraries and even forced librarians and teachers to resign.

The March 1963 issue of this publication described an incident in Lowndes County, Georgia, in which Steinbeck's *East of Eden* was banned by the school board from all school libraries in the county school system, at the instigation of objecting parents.[15] Members of the board admitted that they had not read the book and were taking the word of the parents who described it as "vulgar trash." A group of parents in Edgerton, Wisconsin, demanded that high school students be prohibited from reading *The Ugly American*, *The Catcher in the Rye*, *Brave New World*, *1984*, *Crime and Punishment*, and *Of Mice and Men*.[16] The school board rejected the demands of these parents except in the case of *The Catcher in the Rye* which it had removed from the high school reading list. In order to be prepared for such situations, librarians and teachers should follow the suggestions made in the ALA Council's statement, "How Libraries and Schools can Resist Censorship."[17]

With the urge toward conformity and the fear of publicity, it is far easier for the librarian to be cautious and conservative in selection, conveniently forgetting the democratic principles of the *School Library Bill of Rights* and the "Right to Read" statement of the National Council of Teachers of English. Materials on all sides of an issue are a "must" purchase for the high school library. When students are able to see various sides of the subject of smoking, for example, to participate knowledgeably in the "give and take" of discussion with fellow students, they have the democratic right to reach their own conclusions. Otherwise, we run the risk of producing a generation of "robots" who automatically accept the ideas given to them. Teachers and librarians have the right to choose the materials they think are best for their teaching purposes, and as professional people they must be trusted to do so.

Of help to the selector of books in controversial areas may be the following:

1. Obscenity and brutality in a book of literature are acceptable if they are not there just to shock and amaze. They must contribute directly to the development of the characters and events.

2. Name-calling and stereotype characters in material on race or religion are not acceptable.

3. Material dealing with sex should be simple, accurate, and in good taste.

4. Objectivity is required in material on politics, and all points of view from the extreme left to the extreme right are to be represented in the library's collection.

The school must be prepared for the individual citizen or group which questions certain material. When a school has a carefully written statement of selection policies together with specific procedures for the handling of this problem, administrators and library staff are able to justify, if necessary, each and every piece of material in the library.

Who Chooses the Materials?

For all school personnel, the selection of library materials is a continuous process. The library staff alone cannot be expected to choose all of the materials. If the librarians did so, there might be a tendency to overbalance the collection with materials on subjects the library staff knows best. Since teachers are subject specialists, they have a responsibility to suggest additions in their respective fields and must make recommendations for library materials in those areas. Although professional personnel have access to reviews of some materials, the library staff has many other selection tools to be given to the appropriate teachers, so that they can choose the ones they consider best. Selection is sometimes done by system-wide committees of school subject specialists. In other communities, librarians meet monthly to discuss new books.

A state-wide group of librarians in Massachusetts has met monthly since 1964-65 to review new books for young people. Known as the Young Adults Cooperative Book Review Group of Massachusetts, it is composed of both public and school librarians. Although its chief purpose is to evaluate new books for the use of its own group of librarians, the published reviews which appear periodically can be obtained on a subscription basis by anyone.[18]

Students' recommendations for new library materials must be given serious consideration. As young people use public libraries, buy paperbacks and records, they have definite ideas on materials other teenagers will enjoy. School activity groups such as the chess club, the hot-rodders and the student council can be invited to make suggestions for new materials. Selection as a classroom activity can be a worthwhile project in any subject area. At a high school in Albuquerque, New Mexico, the selection of books in the major subjects covered by the curriculum was a project of two senior English classes. Related subjects were grouped together, and each student chose from five broad subject groups the one in which he wanted to select books. Various book reviewing tools were made available for their use in the classroom as well as in the library. Personal knowledge about certain books was a consideration in the selection. Each group was asked to stay within a certain sum of money, and group agreement had to be reached in the final selections. In addition to helping to choose books, the students learned many other things which gave them a layman's comprehension of the problems a librarian must face in book selection. The existing library collection had to be checked to see what titles the library already had on the subject and consideration given as to whether it would be worthwhile to buy additional copies of certain titles. Other factors about spending the money wisely were considered: quantity *versus* quality, binding, discounts, usability of the books by a limited number or a large group of students. At the completion of the project, a spokesman for each subject group reported to the class on the problems encountered. He gave a brief account of each title chosen, justifying its addition to the library. After the list had been looked over by the librarian, the books were ordered. When they had arrived and were made ready for use, they were put temporarily in a separate place and labeled "New Books Selected by Seniors." A list of the books was made and circulated throughout the school.

The Role of the Library Staff in the Selection Process

However, regardless of who takes part in the selection of new library materials, the professional library staff has final responsibility for what is actually ordered. In addition to giving book lists to school personnel and seeing to it that books are suggested by them, the librarians must look over these recommendations in the light of the existing library collection, so that some sort of balance is maintained. This is no easy task. For instance, an enthusiastic teacher of American history may pressure for new additions to a history collection which is already strong, while teachers in other departments may fail to cooperate in making recommendations for a collection which is already weak. Through the day to day request for information, the librarians are made aware of the shortcomings of certain collections in the library, and they constantly make note of specific needs as they arise. Yet the real problem lies in the extent to which the librarian should yield to requests for the purchase of materials recommended by teachers who encourage their students to make use of materials. In addition, we believe that it is an equal responsibility of the library staff to purchase materials in subject fields not used to the extent they should be, and then to do everything possible to encourage teachers to enrich their teaching by the use of these materials.

There are other reasons why the library staff must have the final "say." Teachers may recommend materials which are really for their own personal use. While it is true that the library maintains a professional collection for its faculty, by far the majority of the materials regularly purchased must be for student use. When teachers recommend additional copies of materials that are already in the library, a decision must be made as to whether this is fair in the light of the total materials budget. The whole problem of balance is considered in relation to the kind of books available in each subject area: "survey" books, "depth" books, books for students who have difficulty reading the basic text, books for the adult reader. What kind of needs are best met with films or other audio-visual material?

In the selection process, the curriculum and the student body of the individual school constantly must be kept in mind. Although various accrediting associations and state departments of education have set up statements as to what percent of the book collection should be in each subject area, these should never be taken at face value, but as loose guides. A high school which has technical and vocational courses would find, for example, that if these percentage statements were followed, the needs of this particular school would not be met.

Expenditures

When schools are committed to the value of the kind of library program described in the preceeding chapters, they will want to spend a considerable amount of money to maintain the program. The library appropriation must be a regular part of the school budget. Gone are the days when school libraries depended on proceeds from the PTA carnival and the generosity of people cleaning their attics of accumulated books. The annual neighborhood drive may have produced a few titles worth putting into the library, but many more were old college texts, Grace Livingston Hill titles, digest books and miscellaneous copies of _Colliers_ and _Jack and Jill_. Libraries which automatically put such material on the shelves obviously believed that any kind of book was better than no books. It is no wonder that the school library of yesterday was sometimes used merely as a study hall or even a place of detention, as it contained an odd assortment of innocuous material bearing no relationship to the curriculum or the students' interests. As material is selected for the modern school library, the pros and cons of each item must be weighed carefully so that the budget is spent wisely.

The cost of library materials is often amazing to the uninitiated. In 1965 the average trade book cost $6. 93 as compared with $6. 55 in 1963 and $5. 81 in 1960. When requesting funds each year, it is a good idea for the library staff to make a brief study of the cost of several individual books today in comparison with the past several years. The same can be done for audiovisual materials and equipment.

How much money is needed for school library materials? The _Standards for School Library Programs_ recommends four to six dollars per pupil as a minimum for regular library books, with additional amounts for reference books, magazines, newspapers and pamphlets. For audiovisual materials, standards recommend a minimum of two to six dollars per pupil. As we look at the cost of library books and audiovisual materials today, these amounts are far too small.

Number of Materials

How many materials does a good school library contain? A minimum collection of 6000 to 10,000 books, or ten books per student, is recommended. One filmstrip for each student in average daily attendance and one hundred recordings are suggested.

New Schools

In the first few years of a new school, careful consideration must be given to the library to see to it that the students have library materials in adequate numbers, to the same degree that they receive adequate textbooks, cafeteria service, etc. Ideally, the library, right from the start, has ten books per student. However, the cost for that number may be an unrealistic amount to have available for trade books alone, from the budget of a new school. A more reasonable plan may be to start with as strong a collection as possible, with a goal of 10,000 volumes by the end of the first three years. In addition, certain reference books, magazines and newspapers are essential right from the beginning. The new school during its first year should have as many filmstrips and recordings as can be obtained, with the goal of one filmstrip per pupil by the end of the third year. Since 16mm films are the most expensive items in the audiovisual field, there may be none purchased during the first year, but six to ten films may be rented. About fifty tape and disc recordings may be a reasonable number to have, with an increase of 150 percent by the end of three years. In addition, some dioramas, study prints, and 8mm films must be available.[19]

In past years as school libraries acquired books through neighborhood book drives, the large number thus obtained may have sounded quite impressive in the school's annual report to the state department of education; but as teachers in today's schools demand many library services and a variety of materials, more and more quality materials must be purchased and more and more money spent.

Other Ways of Obtaining Materials

In addition to obtaining library materials by purchase, some may be rented or borrowed and others received as gifts. Borrowing and renting materials, particularly in audiovisual media, may be the best way to meet a particular library need. Most states have one or more public universities with audiovisual centers which loan or rent their materials throughout the state. In addition, some institutions, such as Indiana University, rent materials to individuals and groups anywhere in the country. Lists and catalogs together with loan regulations are usually available.

Various organizations and businesses also produce materials which can be borrowed on free loan or for the payment of transportation charges. The producers of the material must be carefully evaluated, since their purpose may be primarily promotional. The Borden Dairy Company, Delta Airlines, and the Ford Motor Company loan materials which may be largely advertisements for their products and services. On the other hand, films of the Commission on Safety Education, the American Cancer Society, and the United Nations are both educational and factual and contain little promotional material. Some tools for the selection of books, films, etc. for purchase include also sources for renting and borrowing audiovisual materials. Included in the selection tools in the Appendix of this book are lists compiled particularly for libraries who rent and borrow materials.

Individual teachers who have a special gift will often create audiovisual materials for use in their own classroom. In some school systems, separate studios with trained technicians produce material for use throughout the system. The librarian might consider reproducing some of these materials for his library. The librarian ought also to be alert through the professional "grapevine" to the possibilities of borrowing materials from a local educational television station.

Another source of the non-purchase of materials is through inter-library loan. Through cooperative agreement, libraries within one community or area borrow materials from each other. In past years, many small schools in rural areas would have had no library materials at all, if it were not for the state library service or the inter-library loan idea.

Another source of non-purchase of materials is from gifts. The circumstances under which gifts are accepted must be decided by the school library in consultation with the administration. Gifts of any kind of library materials are accepted with the understanding that if the library has no use for them, they will be given to other libraries or individuals who can use them. The same standards that the library applies to purchased material apply to gifts. Parent-teacher groups and student organizations sometimes give money to the library. If these groups want the money spent for materials in a particular subject or of a particular kind, they ought to consult with the library staff who will give them specific suggestions or selection tools. In one high school known to the writer, the local chapter of the National Honor Society gave money during three successive years for the purchase of materials for college-bound students. Each year the Society appointed a committee to consult with the librarians on the selection of books in certain subject areas. These varied from year to year. The Society chose a bookplate which was put into each book, identifying the donors. In the same school, the student council gave the library money for books in memory of a student who tragically had been killed. The Council asked that books on aviation be purchased, as it had been the student's particular interest. A committee helped with the selection, and the art department designed a bookplate to be used in the books.

Most requests made of the library will be answered through the permanent library collection which is maintained by regular purchase and occasionally supplemented by gifts. However, an important and necessary library service is accomplished by borrowing and renting material to meet the needs of students and teachers.

Weeding the Collection

Just as new materials are added, old ones need to be discarded so that the library is always a live, working collection. Both print and non-print materials which are beyond repair should be disposed of. Materials which have ideas that have been superceded by new developments are outmoded. People in old-fashioned clothing appearing in films or filmstrips often are simply a source of humor with the students. Sometimes a library has books in its collection that have never been used because they have proved to be inappropriate for that library. If they can be made use of by other libraries in the school system or the community, they should be given to them.

Books which have not been used because of their unattractive appearance--often old editions of classics--should be replaced by attractive editions. When a library has multiple copies of books once used extensively--often because a certain title was required reading for a particular teacher no longer in the school--all but one copy should be removed. At some time in the library's history, volumes of series books not considered acceptable reading for young people, such as the Cherry Ames nursing stories, may have crept into the collection. These should be discarded. A suggested list of such series was compiled by the Michigan State Library and appears in the pamphlet _Weeding the Small Library Collection._[20] When a librarian knows books well, there is nothing immoral or wanton about weeding the collection. The pamphlet file, by the temporary nature of its contents which may appear later in book form, should be thoroughly weeded every two years.

Only through regular and continuous weeding can each item in the library be of potential use to its patrons.

Acquisition Procedures

As materials are recommended, each title is placed on a card giving as much information about it as is then known, plus the name of the person suggesting it and any explanation as to the purpose for which it is recommended. When the titles have been found in some review media, bookstore, exhibit, etc., that fact is also noted, plus the date the card was made. Regular printed cards suitable for this use are available from numerous library supply houses.

When and how often orders for library materials are to be placed may be a decision made by the school's administration and business office. Once a year is not often enough, as this does not allow for unexpected additions needed when new courses are added, losses of basic materials experienced, sudden increases in enrollment, and for newly produced materials. Probably dates set twice each semester is best.

As the time approaches when library orders are to be placed, announcements to that effect are made to faculty and students about four weeks prior to the date, so that last minute suggestions can be made. However, the continuous "consideration file" will likely be the major source of possible acquisitions. As the library staff looks over the file, there are many points to be considered or checked before final decisions are reached. For books, all titles in the file must be checked in the latest annual volume Books in Print, or the latest annual and quarterly issues of Cumulative Book Index to get the complete information for each title which is necessary before placing an order: author's full name, complete title, edition, publisher, publication date, list price. When new book reviewing guides are checked regularly, this information may already be on the consideration card. In such cases, it can be considered accurate. When a book is not listed in the latest volume of Books in Print and is not located in a recently published selection tool or publisher's catalog, it usually can be considered out of print and therefore cannot be obtained from regular sources. When teachers have recommended books which are no longer in print, they should be informed of this fact.

If the library staff and others note library needs and make recommendations throughout the year, there will be more titles in the consideration file than there is money to spend at any one order time. Cards for materials not ordered are kept in the consideration file for review at the time of the next order.

As complete information on most of the possible additions is obtained, the library staff looks them over, considering each one in relation to the money now to be spent and the known library needs. If it has not previously been done, each title is checked against the card catalog. If copies of the item are found to be already in the library, the question of the advisability of added copies is considered.

As the library staff sorts through the cards from the consideration file, numerous other factors are kept in mind: balance of the total collection and balance within each subject field, recentness of the item in relation to the subject matter, kinds of bindings, individual prices, which medium--film, book, recording, etc.--is best to meet the specific need.

In some subject areas, it will be found that pamphlets are to be preferred over books or audiovisual material. For example, pamphlets on careers are preferable because the information in them is apt to be more up to date. At low cost, the career pamphlets can be replaced and updated every two or three years.

Where and How Materials are Ordered

Although the school's business office may make the final decision as to where materials are ordered, librarians must be knowledgeable on this subject so that they can give suggestions concerning new developments which will affect this decision. As new school libraries are established or purchases increased, a thorough investigation of the possibilities must be made, so that the best possible service is obtained. Materials are usually ordered from one or all of the following sources: directly from each publisher or producer, from a book jobber, from local bookstores and audiovisual suppliers. A number of factors enter into the decision concerning the placement of orders. Since jobbers have in stock the publications of many publishers, they are apt to be preferred over the individual publisher. Also, much less bookkeeping is involved. In an order for a thousand dollars worth of books, it is highly possible that thirty or thirty-five publishers are represented. The placing of orders and the payment of bills to each one necessitates a great deal of record-keeping. When jobbers give prompt and accurate service, inform librarians when titles will be delayed or are not available, and will put special bindings on some or all of the books as indicated by the library, orders through them are apt to be filled very satisfactorily. A flat thirty percent discount from a jobber can be considered good, while discounts will vary with each publisher, from a minimum of ten percent to as much as forty percent. On the other hand, an individual publisher will probably give faster service for a rush order. Buying materials through a local supplier can be good public relations for a school system. It also has the advantage of convenience and may allow the library staff to examine the materials before purchase.

In recent years, largely because of federal appropriations, book orders have flooded the publishing industry, sometimes causing delays and mistakes in distribution. A study aimed at isolating and suggesting solutions for some of these problems was begun in October 1966, under the sponsorship of the American Library Association and the National League of Cities.

A word must be said about the careful and accurate typing of the actual orders. A separate order for each type of materials, i.e., books, films, filmstrips, recordings, is required. The cards will need to be reshuffled in the order desired. Whether the publisher or the jobber wants the list arranged alphabetically by title or author must be found out. Some jobbers will prefer to have the list in order by publisher, and alphabetically by author within each publisher's group. Two or more copies of the order need to be made, with the following information for each item requested: number of copies, author (in the case of books), title, edition, publisher, price. The original copy is mailed to the jobber or publisher, another copy is kept by the library, and others may be sent to the school's principal or the central business office. The consideration or order cards are put back into alphabetical order by author, awaiting the arrival of the books and other materials. This is now known as the file of orders outstanding.

Decisions on what magazines the library should subscribe to are controlled largely by the ordering, on an automatic renewal basis, of magazines in the Reader's Guide to Periodical Literature. Other magazines received should be reviewed annually for deletions or additions to the order list. All of them are best ordered through one reliable magazine agency. Subscriptions to newspapers may be combined with the annual magazine order, or they are ordered directly from the publishers.

Pamphlets are usually ordered in two different ways. Some may be ordered on a subscription basis. For example, a library may want to receive all of the career monographs of the Institute for Research or all of the guidance publications of Science Research Associates as they are published during the year. Other pamphlets may be ordered every three or four months directly from their source, to be paid for from the library's fine fund.

The ordering process requires the following of certain procedures and routines. When it is done in careful and accurate fashion, the library can be assured of receiving most of the items ordered.

Notes

1. A complete copy can be obtained free from The American Association of School Librarians, 50 East Huron Street, Chicago, Illinois. 60611

2. See Appendix I for excerpts.

3. *Librarian's Handbook,* Shoreline School District No. 412, Seattle, Washington, 1965, p. 62.

4. Books on Exhibit, Mount Kisco, New York. 10549

5. Combined Paperback Exhibit, Briarcliff Manor, New York. 10510

6. See Appendix II for selected lists.

7. Everett L. Moore, "Processing Center for California Junior College Libraries - A Preliminary Study," *Library Resources and Technical Services* IX (Summer, 1965), 303-317.

8. *Ulrich's International Periodicals Directory*, 11th edition, R. R. Bowker Co., 1965.

9. See Appendix II for selected list.

10. *Audio Cardalog*, Box 989, Larchmont, New York. 10538

11. Educational Film Library Association, Inc., 250 W. 57th St., New York. 10019

12. James W. Brown and Richard B. Lewis, *A-V Instructional Materials Manual*, 2nd edition, McGraw-Hill, 1964.

13. *The Teachers' Library; How to Organize it and What to Include*, National Education Association, 1966.

14. Marjorie Fiske, *Book Selection and Censorship; A Study of School and Public Libraries in California*, Berkeley: University of California Press, 1959.

15. "Where They Ban the Better Books They Maim the Better Minds," *Newsletter on Intellectual Freedom*, XII (March, 1963), 21.

16. *Ibid.*

17. See Appendix III for a copy of this statement.

18. *Book Reviews*, Mrs. Leila-Jane Roberts, Winchester Public Library, Winchester, Massachusetts. 01890

19. See Appendix IV for detailed statements of quantitative standards.

20. *Weeding the Small Library Collection*, Small Libraries Project Pamphlet No. 5 Suppl. A, American Library Association, 1962.

Selected Audiovisual Materials

Book Banning. 16mm film. sound, black and white, 14 min. 1957. Accompanying handbook. (See It Now Series) Produced by CBS-TV. McGraw-Hill Text Film Corp.

The Consitution and Censorship. 16mm film, sound, black and white. 29 min. (Decision Series) Available from Indiana University, Audio-Visual Center, Bloomington, Indiana. 47401

Now and Forever. 16mm film. sound, color, 14 min. 1964. University Microfilms, 300 N. Zeeb Rd., Ann Arbor, Michigan. 48106

Value of using microfilm to preserve books and other materials.

Available on loan for round-trip shipping charges from Headquarters Library, American Library Association, 50 East Huron Street, Chicago, Illinois. 60611

Paperback Books in Your School. Filmstrip. sound, color, 15 min. Produced by the Bureau of Independent Publishers and Distributors. Obtain for free use from your local BIPAD member wholesaler.

Selection and Use of Programmed Materials. Filmstrip. color, 15 min. 1964. Accompanying handbook. National Education Association, 1206 Sixteenth St. N.W., Washington, D.C. 20036

Selected Readings

Selection Principles and Policies

Blackshear, Martha Jule. _School Administrators Ask Leading Questions about Library Materials._ Montgomery, Alabama: State Department of Education, 1961. (pamphlet)

Book Selection Policies. 2nd ed. Baltimore, Maryland: Enoch Pratt Free Library, 1961. (pamphlet)

Carter, M.D. and W. J. Bonk. _Building Library Collections._ 2nd ed. The Scarecrow Press, Inc., 1964.

Case, E. R. "Critical Book Selection," _Illinois Libraries_, XLVI (April, 1964), 291-294.

Craig, Anne and John Rowell. "What Books for the Young Adult?" _Library Journal_, LXXXIX (October 15, 1964), 4103-4106.

Cushman, Jerome. "The Hidden Persuaders in Book Selection," _Library Journal_, XC (September 15, 1965), 3553-3558.

Danton, J. P., ed. The Climate of Book Selection; Social Influences on School and Public Libraries. Berkeley; University of California School of Librarianship, 1959.

Erbes, Raymond G. "Developing a Basic Collection of Library Microfilms, Microfiche, Micro-opaque and Filmstrips," American School Board Journal, CLI (November, 1965), 28-31.

________. "Microfilm can Increase Space, Update Services," American School Board Journal, CLIII (December, 1966), 28-31.

Gaver, Mary V. and Marian Scott. Evaluating Library Resources for Elementary School Libraries. (Elementary School Library Series No. 1) New Brunswick, New Jersey: SSH Press, 1962.

Heidbreder, M. A. "Partners in Book Selection," [Publishers and Librarians] School Libraries, XIV (March, 1965), 21-29.

Instructional Materials: Selection Policies and Procedures. California Association of School Librarians, n. d. (pamphlet)

Limbacher, J. L. "Film Evaluation and Criticism," ALA Bulletin, LVIII (January, 1964), 43-47.

MacQuown, V. J. and V. Westphal. "The Teenage Novel," Library Journal, LXXXIX (April 15, 1964), 1832-1835.

Miller, Marilyn and Margaret Oliver. I Want to Buy Books for the School Library but...! Topeka, Kansas: Kansas State Department of Public Education, 1964. (pamphlet)

Nordstrom, Ursula. "Honesty in Teenage Novels," Top of the News, XXI (November, 1964), 35-38.

Schindel, Morton, "Confessions of a Book Fiend," Library Journal, XCII (February 15, 1967), 858-859.

White, Dana Lee. "Government Publications: Much for Little," School Libraries, XIII (May, 1964), 43-48.

Wofford, Azile. Book Selection for School Libraries. The H. W. Wilson Co., 1962.

How Materials are Chosen

Burress, Lee A., Jr. "Role of the Teacher in Selecting Library Books," Education, LXXXVI (March, 1966), 398-403.

Davidson, D. L. "Books for Poor Readers in High School?" Education, LXXXVII (November, 1966), 164-166.

Galloway, M. L. An Analytical Study of the Extent and Nature of the Reviewing of Juvenile Books in Eight Journals and Newspapers with Special Regard to their Usefulness as Selection Aids for School Libraries. Ed. D. Dissertation, Columbia University, 1965. Available on microfilm from University Microfilms, 300 N. Zeeb Rd., Ann Arbor, Michigan. 48106

Gerhardt, L. N. "Young Adult Reviewing at Kirkus," Top of the News, XX (December, 1963), 111-113.

Hektoen, Faith. "State-wide Book Reviewing Project; the Inaugural Year," Top of the News, XXII (January, 1966), 200-202.

How to Collect Free and Inexpensive Materials. (pamphlet) Available from Mrs. Alicia Huff, Burbank Public Library, Burbank, California. 91501

"Index of Audiovisual Reviews," Audiovisual Instruction, XLIV (September, 1965), 596-604.

Leonard, V. "Book Selection in Grosse Pointe: Where School Librarians Advise the Public Library," ALA Bulletin, LX (June, 1966), 627-629.

Limbacher, J. L. "Film Evaluation and Criticism," ALA Bulletin, LVIII (January, 1964), 43-48.

Solomon, Albert E. "AIM - A Year Later," Audiovisual Instruction, XII (January, 1967), 39-40.

Describes a state-wide film evaluation project undertaken in New York.

Problems in Selection

Agree, R. H. "Freedom to Read on Long Island," Top of the News, XXII (April, 1966), 285-287.

Ahrens, N. H. Censorship and the Teachers of English: A Questionnaire Survey of a Selected Sample of Secondary School Teachers of English. Ed.D. dissertation, Columbia University, 1965. Available on microfilm from University Microfilms, 300 N. Zeeb Rd., Ann Arbor, Michigan. 48106

Burress, Lee A., Jr. How Censorship Affects the School. Special Bulletin No. 8, October 1963. Oshkosh, Wisconsin: Wisconsin Council of Teachers of English. (pamphlet)

Combating Undemocratic Pressures on Schools and Libraries: A Guide for Local Communities. New York: American Civil Liberties Union, 1964. (pamphlet)

"Controversies in Selection," Top of the News, XXII (April, 1966).

Six articles.

Downs, Robert, Ed. The First Freedom: Liberty and Justice in the World of Books and Reading. Chicago: American Library Association, 1960.

Edwards, R. L. and Katharine Keathley. "Magazines for Boys - Recent Research and Selection Problems," Top of the News, XX (March, 1964), 227-230.

Freedom of Inquiry: Supporting the Library Bill of Rights. Conference on Intellectual Freedom Proceedings, January 23-24, 1965. Chicago: American Library Association.

Gaines, Ervin J. "The Library Bill of Rights," Library Journal, XCII (March 1, 1967), 984-985.

Gothberg, Helen. "Y A Censorship: Adult or Adolescent Problem?" Top of the News, XXII (April, 1966), 275-278.

Hogan, Robert F. "Book Selection and Censorship," National Association of Secondary School Principals Bulletin. LI (April, 1967), 67-77.

Intellectual Freedom Kit. New Edition. Berkeley: California Library Association, 1966.

Knudson, Rozanne. "My Mother, the Censor," ALA Bulletin, LX (June, 1966), 613-616.

Parker, T. F. "Book Selection for the Culturally Deprived," Library Journal, LXXXIX (September 15, 1964), 3260-3265.

"Problems in Book Selection for Children," Drexel Library Quarterly, January, 1966. (entire issue)

The Students' Right to Read. Champaign, Illinois: National Council of Teachers of English, 1962. (pamphlet)

Paperbacks

Bass, J. A. and others. "How to Set up a Paperback Bookstore," School Management, VI (August, 1962), 25-26+

Beauchamp, R., ed. "Paperbacks, A Symposium," Scholastic Teacher, LXXXIII (January 17, 1964), 21T-35T.

Bourgeois, Y. P. and D. Lilley. "Blueprint for Paperbacks in the High School Library," Library Journal, LXXXVIII (January, 1963), 270-271+

French, W. "First Year of the Paperback Revolution," College

English, XXV (January, 1964), 255-260.

Larrick, Nancy. "When You Buy a Book You Read It," Library Journal, LXXXVI (January 15, 1961), 338-339.

"Paperbacks," Library Journal, XC (January, 1965), 297-313. (series of articles)

Schiller, H. "Panel Urges Schools to Incorporate Paperbacks; Striking Cases Cited," Library Journal, LXXXVIII (February, 1963), 844-845.

Cost of Materials

"The Cost of Audio-Visual Instruction," Product Information for Schools, V (3rd Quarter, 1966), 21-22.

Dane, C. "School Library Book Budget," Focus, (May, 1965), 34-36.

Robinson, Margaret M. The School Library Budget; A Handbook for Beginning Librarians. Ann Arbor Michigan: Edwards Bros., 1964.

Acquisition Procedures

Wulfekoetter, G. Acquisition Work: Processes Involved In Building Library Collections. Seattle: University of Washington, 1962.

Chapter VII

Processing and Circulating of Materials

After new library materials have been selected and ordered, they must be organized properly in order that maximum use can be attained. The importance of good cataloging and classification so that related materials are shelved together by subject, and users are guided to them through the catalog, cannot be denied.

There are three possibilities for processing new materials: (1) through centralized processing in the school system or cooperatively with public or school libraries within a geographical area, (2) through commercial sources, (3) in the local school.

Centralized Processing

The establishment of a center for the processing of library materials for all the schools in one district or system has been done more and more in recent years. A number of school districts which have added centralized processing have been influenced in their decision to do so by the recommendation of the American Association of School Librarians which states in its Standards for School Library Programs:

> Centralized technical processing constitutes a form of cooperative planning for school libraries that takes place before the establishment of a materials center. When school systems have three or more schools, centralized processing should be introduced.[1]

Some centers process materials completely, including the preparation of all catalog cards, the pasting in of pockets and date-due slips, typing book cards, and preparing spine labels. Those centers which only catalog the materials may do so on the theory that local library staffs are more apt to become acquainted with the materials when they are responsible for the pockets, etc. The central service may be given only to the elementary schools in a system because there are sometimes fewer professional librarians serving in the elementary schools. The center may process only books.

Baltimore Schools

An account of the background for establishment of a centralized processing service and the first five years of its existence in the Baltimore Public Schools shows that during the first twenty months, 166,373 books were handled by the Department at a processing cost of fifty-two cents per book.[2] In addition to processing books purchased from regular appropriations, the Central Cataloging Department provided catalog cards, book pockets, etc. for books acquired by the local schools from fine funds, gift money, and other sources. After thorough study of various methods for reproducing cards, it was decided to use a Multilith machine. Electric typewriters and an electric pasting machine were among the first items of equipment purchased. Although it was recognized that there were disadvantages to centralized processing, the Baltimore schools felt that after five years of the Centralized Cataloging Department's existence, the following were among the many advantages realized:[3]

1. Better quality of cataloging
2. Uniformity and consistency in classification and subject headings
3. Better cataloging for more schools, including those without librarians
4. Local librarians had more time to work with students and teachers when they were relieved of the technical processes
5. Books appeared on shelves sooner
6. Provided for expansion of library service to include audiovisual materials

Albuquerque Schools

A more recently established processing center is the one for the Albuquerque, New Mexico, Public Schools. In March, 1964, when the Center began its service, books for new elementary schools starting their collections were given priority. Then the processing of books for the older elementary schools was added, followed by service to new secondary schools, and finally the older secondary schools. Centralized ordering for all schools was added in the early stages of the Center. Because of the great increase in volume of work, the quarters for the Center have been greatly expanded and more and larger IBM equipment has been added. A total of 48,550 titles were processed in 1966 for 101 schools. The processing of supplementary texts and of filmstrips was begun during the same year, and plans are being made for the processing of recordings. In 1966-67 the staff consisted of three librarians, eleven clerks, and four additional part-time personnel who were working in the Center itself. There were five additional people who worked exclusively with Center's data processing equipment.[4]

Another possibility is for centralized processing by a number of school districts coperating in the establishment of a single center, or establishment by school and public libraries in one area. Although this kind of cooperation exists in the public library field, little has been done among school districts.

The advantages of centralized processing include: cataloging done by experts, each one specializing in a particular task, single purchase of cataloging tools and equipment, use of machines, purchase of books and supplies in large quantities allowing for better prices, release of local library staff's time to aid teachers and students.

Commercial Processing

The second way in which new books may be processed is by using the services of commercial companies. The two major commercial sources best suited for school library books are Lj Cards, Inc., P. O. Box 27, Cooper Station Post Office, New York 10036 (a subsidiary of R. R. Bowker Co.,) and Bro-Dart Books, Inc., P. O. Box 923, Williamsport, Penn. 17701. From Lj Cards, Inc., can be obtained for twenty-nine cents per book a kit containing eight printed catalog cards, reinforced book pocket, book card, and vinyl spine label imprinted with call number. These kits are available for all titles listed in Publishers Library Bindings in Print which is the annual Bowker catalog that lists books obtainable in publishers' reinforced bindings. In Bro-Dart's 1966 catalog of books and audiovisual materials there are over 26,000 titles listed for which processing can be obtained in any of these ways: (1) books themselves can be purchased completely processed, (2) books can be ordered together with the processing and cataloging kit for each one, (3) processing and cataloging kits alone. There are some book jobbers, including H. R. Huntting Co. and A. C. McClurg and Co., from which the library can obtain kits at the same time books are ordered. Some commercial outlets prepare processing kits according to a library's specifications or on a standardized plan at a cost varying from seventy-five cents to one dollar and seventy-five cents per book. As school districts contract to buy large numbers of books preprocessed, the cost may be as low as sixty-five cents per book.[5]

Local Processing

Finally we come to the time-consuming task of processing materials in the local library. All kinds of supplies must be purchased for preparing books to be circulated: catalog cards, book pockets and cards, date-due slips, labels or stylus and transfer paper, paste brushes, etc. A good source for finding the names of all kinds of library supplies and equipment is the annual listing which appears in the Library Journal. The quarterly publication, Product Information for Schools (The Management Publishing Group, 22 W. Putnam Ave., Greenwich, Conn. 06830) lists new supplies and equipment under various subjects of interest to librarians including: Books; Audio-Visual Accessories; Curriculum Aids; Films, Filmstrips and Slides; Projectors and Screens; Teaching Machines.

The use of printed catalog cards which have been available for many years from the H. W. Wilson Company and the Library of Congress is a service which no school library can afford to neglect using. Wilson cards are available for most of the books purchased by the school library. Practically all American publications have printed on the verso of the title page the order number for obtaining the book's Library of Congress catalog cards. Since the cards produced by the Library of Congress have been, in the past, ones for adult books primarily, only large school libraries or those having a high concentration of adult books have obtained cards from that source. However, in 1966 the LC Card Division began providing catalog cards for juvenile books, with these cards being somewhat different from the usual pattern of LC cards. Fewer subdivisions are used for subject headings, and a summary is included. Whether or not to mix cards from Wilson and the Library of Congress must be considered. When cards are purchased from both sources, there will be very few problems with the Dewey classification numbers except that LC cards may assign a longer Dewey numbers than the Wilson cards, but it is easy to shorten them. But in the matter of subject headings, for many of the adult books there can be considerable difference in the wording of headings for the same subject. Hence, it may be best to purchase LC cards without the subject headings printed on them. But for the most part, Wilson and LC cards are very satisfactory used exactly as they are. One good reason for using these cards is the satisfaction of knowing that they are expertly prepared. Another is that when cards are purchased, the processing of new books is completed more quickly, allowing the extra time thus released for work with students and teachers.

A service of some publishers is the provision of catalog cards with their books, usually sets produced by Wilson or the Library of Congress. This is particularly helpful for those libraries which order books directly from publishers rather than through a wholesale distributor or jobber, as they can count on receiving the catalog cards from certain ones.

Even though a school obtains printed cards for many of its books, there will always be some which must be fully cataloged by the library staff. Any and all professional aids should be used. The Wilson Company's *Standard Catalog for High School Libraries* with its annual supplements, and the 1965 publication, *Junior High School Library Catalog,* are primarily book selection tools, but since each title is fully described and classification numbers and subject headings are given, these publications are of great help to the cataloger. The *American Book Publishing Record* (monthly accumulation of the "Weekly Record" of the *Publisher's Weekly*) is of similar assistance.

The assigning of numbers to books in the order in which they are acquired by a library and entering certain order information about each title in an accession book is not advocated. After many years of using these accession numbers as a part of the processing of new books, most school libraries have decided that they serve no real purpose. The information giving source, cost and date of purchase, originally appearing in the accession book, is now put on each book's shelf list card.

The assigning of Cutter numbers--also called book numbers--following the author's initial and placed under the Dewey number is not recommended for school libraries. The most common practice is to use the first three letters of the author's last name, under the class number.

Paperbacks

Whether or not to catalog paperback books is another decision to be made. When paperbacks were first purchased by libraries, the tendency was to shelve them separately from the rest of the collection and to leave them uncataloged. As libraries became aware of the valuable books published in so-called "soft" covers, they cataloged them fully and shelved them along with the other books.

Cataloging Audiovisual Materials

Although there are many aids for the cataloging of library books, the same cannot be said for non-book materials. There is some possibility that in the near future, producers of the most commonly purchased audio-visual materials will provide catalog cards as do some book publishers. Audio Cardalog cards and EFLA Film Evaluations, although chiefly an aid in selecting audiovisual materials, can be used as main entries or to assist in cataloging. Isolated cases exist where catalog cards are sent along with the purchase of prints. For example, Bro-Dart Industries includes cards with their Master Colorprints. Meanwhile, the library staff processing non-print materials uses the same principles of descriptive cataloging as are used for books. A major administrative decision must be made, however, on whether or not to assign class numbers to non-print materials. Some libraries use the appropriate Dewey number according to the subject matter of the item, adding a symbol which indicates the type of material, i. e., FS (for filmstrip), K (for kit), RE (for recording). Others omit Dewey numbers and use a combination of symbols and accession numbers. Probably the latter is the most common practice today.

Magazines, pamphlets and pictures are usually not cataloged in school libraries. Back issues of magazines are arranged alphabetically by title with a visible tab or card file readily accessible, giving title and dates of each magazine. The back issues are available on microfilm in many of the more progressive school libraries. The microfilm rolls are kept in cabinets with the reading machines necessary for their use located nearby. Pamphlets and pictures are filed together or separately in a legal size vertical filing cabinet, arranged by subject. A card referring to the vertical file is typed for each subject and is included in the catalog.

A record of all materials which the library owns are found in one alphabetical arrangement in the card catalog. Cards for non-book material may be of a different color or may have a colored band for each form, i.e., red for filmstrips, blue for records, white for books, etc. Numerous cross reference cards, including those suggested in the Sears _List of Subject Headings_ and ones to meet special needs of most school libraries, must be entered in the catalog.

Book Catalogs

Although the move toward catalogs in book form has gained momentum in recent years largely in university libraries and to some extent in public libraries, it appears not to be used in school libraries. In a school which already has Zerox-type machines, the task of reproduction and its expense would not be as great as otherwise. Teachers would see a great advantage in having on their desks a copy of the library's catalog to which they and their students could refer immediately as the need arose. Copies could be made available at strategic places throughout the school plant. As schools loan library books to each other, the book catalog would be an easy way to see if another library had the titles one needed. Tysee sees both advantages and disadvantages in the use of printed book catalogs.[6] Among the disadvantages she points out are: possible great expense; impossibility of having it up-to-date with the new acquisitions; necessity for consulting more than one alphabet (because supplements as well as the original catalog have to be consulted); more apt to be mutilated, marked, and quickly worn out than cards in the catalog. Tysee includes the following among the advantages: allows for use anywhere, not confined to a fixed place; multiple copies can be made;

visually superior; easier to make bibliographies from it; condenses space; serves as a resource tool for a library system. The use of book catalogs seems highly practical from the service point of view for a school library, provided they are supplementary to the card catalog, not substitutes for it.

The catalog in the school library must be a means to an end, not an end in itself. Its chief purpose is to guide students and teachers to the contents of the library. School librarians are about one hundred percent in agreement that materials should be on open shelves, easy to get at for reference and browsing. Yet they may do the kind of cataloging that holds the student at the catalog, attempting to figure out all of the detailed information given in the entries, when he should use it largely to get the location (call numbers) of material so that he can go immediately to the shelves and examine the material directly. Only in libraries of 100,000 volumes or more where the time consumed in locating materials can be great, or in libraries with closed stacks does detailed information on catalog cards have value. Nor is there much need for cards under illustrators, joint authors, and series. Posters giving examples of various ways subjects are entered should be near the catalog, as should examples of the way the cards are filed. Students can be encouraged to buy a library guide to use as a ready reference to the card catalog and the arrangement of materials, such as the one prepared by Donald Cook and Hilda Grieder of Columbia University.[7] Many students simply avoid using the card catalog because it seems very complicated to them. Every effort should be made to make it as simple as possible, and yet be a valuable, accurate, and up-to-date record of the library's contents.

Cataloging Aids

One of the finest aids to the librarian who administers technical services in the school library is a "Checklist of Individual Library Practices" appearing in the appendix of Piercy's book, Commonsense Cataloging.[8] Here is a detailed listing of practices of libraries concerning the card catalog, main entry cards, added entries, the shelf list, non-book and near-book materials, and others, which are to be checked as done by an individual library. As well as checking the practice followed in a particular library, these listings can be used to indicate which tasks are to be performed by clerical personnel. Other valuable appendices include a selected list of library publishers and suppliers, a list of library terms, rules for alphabetical filing, and directions for typing all kinds of catalog cards. Miss Piercy's manual is one which school librarians will find very useful. Other recommended manuals for technical processes in school libraries are listed in the "Selected Readings" at the end of this chapter.

Studies and Research

Although a number of school systems have written accounts of particular procedures being used in centralized processing, very little research is available on technical services particularly in the school library. A 1942 study on costs is far too old to be of value today.[9] A study made to find out the amount of time spent by school librarians on clerical duties in connection with cataloging and the average time necessary to catalog a book was conducted in California.[10] The conclusion was reached that school librarians spend too much time on jobs that could be done by clerks. Since this study was made in 1959 and used only ten books, its conclusions are limited and debatable.

After library materials have been cataloged and prepared for the shelves, decisions have to be made on how they are to be shelved and on procedures for their circulation. Should each medium be shelved separately or most media placed together by subject? Especially when filmstrips, recordings, and other audiovisual material have Dewey class numbers on them, it seems easy to shelve them along with the books which have the same Dewey numbers. Pamphlets can be put in boxes rather than in vertical files and shelved with the other material on a subject. This arrangement of most learning materials may appear to be the most valuable and practical for teachers and students; for here in one area can be seen everything the library has on a subject, with the exception of magazine and newspaper information and certain realia. When a borrower looks up a subject in the catalog and finds listed there all the material available regardless of its format, it seems logical for him to find all of it shelved together, rather than having to go to different areas of the library to see each medium. But the non-print materials cannot be examined right at the shelves as books can. In order to listen to a recording or to preview a filmstrip, the potential borrower will have to go to some other part of the library where recorders and viewers are located. Also the practical necessity of having a number of different sizes of shelves in one area is likely to arise. Hence it may work out better to have audiovisual materials in a place separate from the books. Careful thought to present and future needs must be given to decisions concerning shelving and location.

Circulation

A number of possibilities arise in connection with circulation procedures. Books, albums of phonograph records, mounted pictures, and kits can have pockets pasted in, with cards in the pockets in a uniform place. But check-out cards for filmstrips, tapes, transparencies, and films will need to be kept in files and the proper card obtained for each item when someone wants to borrow it, with different colored check-out cards for each kind of material. For borrowing uncataloged materials, i. e., magazines, pamphlets, unmounted pictures, single maps, a form card adaptable for any of this material can be used. This card has space for filling in the type of material, title or subject of the item, number of items, signature and room number of the borrower, and the date due. The traditional method of checking out material in the school library is for the borrower to sign his name and number on the check-out card. However, a few school libraries are using charging machines. One machine which has been suggested as practical for school libraries is the Sysdac charging machine.[11] Each borrower has a plastic library card containing his name and address. The book card and the borrower's card are inserted into the machine. A strip of pressurized tape indicating date due and the borrower's name and address become affixed to the book card. On one end of this tape there is a perforated tab which is removed and placed in the book pocket as a "date due" reminder. When books are returned, this tab is removed from the book and also from the book card which is in the charge file.

Kager sees the following advantages in using the Sysdac charging machine: the book card never has to be replaced as it is never used up; sending of overdue notices is facilitated; when a borrower forgets his library card a blank one can be inserted in the machine and the borrower can sign the tape.[12]

Decisions must be made concerning length of time materials can be borrowed and the number of items that can be taken at one time. This is apt to vary with the kind of material and whether it is being borrowed by students or faculty. Students may borrow books for two weeks; pamphlets for one week; filmstrips and recordings for three days. Regulations concerning the number of items which can be borrowed by students is apt to vary with the kind of material and the size of the collection in relation to the number of students in the school. If a library has 25,000 books or more to serve 2,000 students, there may be no limit to the number borrowed. Even in such a large collection there may be a regulation that not more than five books on the same subject can be checked out at a time. This may be necessary because frequently there are apt to be many students studying a particular aspect of a course at the same time, so that there is heavy demand in one area during a certain period of time. Libraries which have small collections of well-used recordings may have to limit their circulation to one day, until more are added. Magazines and reference books may circulate to students only overnight. Teachers should have more lenient privileges than students. It is not unusual for them to be able to borrow books for as long as a month or a semester. However, the library always reserves the right to call in materials which are on long loans to teachers, when there are requests for specific items or the material is needed for special reserve shelves. Since much of the audiovisual material together with the equipment necessary for its use is borrowed by teachers for classroom use, the length of time it is to be borrowed varies according to need. A large wall calendar on which teachers can sign in advance for specific material is practical. This chart or calendar provides a place to write in the title, call number, and medium (filmstrip, kit, etc.), together with the teacher's name and room number, on each date the item is desired.

Circulation Files

How cards for materials in circulation are to be filed must be decided. Some librarians prefer that they be filed by the date the materials are due, especially when overdue notices are made out daily. Others think that filing all cards by call number is preferable, because this means that when a member of the library staff is trying to find out who has a particular item, only one place in the file needs to be checked. Which ever way is chosen, cards for each medium are filed separately; thus there is one file of cards for books, another for filmstrips, and so on. Separate files may be kept for teachers' loans. Records of what books and magazines are at the bindery must also be kept at the circulation desk.

Circulation of Equipment

Keeping track of the equipment necessary for use with audio-visual materials is another task of the circulation aspect of the library. Each item is identified by simply marking each one with a consecutive accession number, and check-out cards are attached or are in a separate file of check-out cards for equipment. An interesting plan for recording where any piece of equipment is at a given time was made up at the Deerfield, Illinois, High School.[13] A floor plan was made of the school and magnets of various colors denoting the type of equipment was placed on the "square" for each room which has such equipment on loan. As each one is returned, the magnet is removed from the square and placed at the bottom of the floor plan. Thus one can tell quickly just where each piece of equipment is. A variation of that plan is to have a weekly equipment-scheduling board with columns across the top representing each class period and the days of the week. Down the left side are the names and numbers of the various pieces of equipment. Nails are in place opposite each one. The name and room number of the teacher requesting a certain projector or recorder is written on a tag which is then hung on the appropriate nail.

Circulation Records

After materials have been properly processed and shelved, they are ready for use. Since practically all of the materials can be borrowed, the question comes up as to whether or not circulation records should be kept. If such records are to be made, they must have a purpose. One factor to be considered as new materials are selected is the extent to which the various parts of the library's collection is used; consequently circulation statistics will be of value here. In examining circulation figures for the preceeding school year, the library staff may discover that an area in which the library has a large and presumably carefully selected collection has been used very little. This gives the staff an idea as to which teachers may need in-service training; the contents of this part of the library's collection may need to be publicized or new approaches to their use discovered. The total number of items circulated each month may show the staff in which month they can expect the heaviest circulation in the coming year. The light use of pamphlets, recordings, etc. may indicate that the circulation regulations for these materials are too restrictive. An interesting item to include in the head librarian's annual report to the principal is the average number of books and other materials borrowed per pupil during the year.

The hours when the library is open and restrictions as to how students are able to come to the library during the school day will affect circulation. When a library is open only during the hours that the school is in session, some students may never or seldom get to the library. The library should be open at least half an hour before school begins and remain open at least an hour after classes are dismissed. This may vary with the location of the school and the school bus schedule. When students are restricted to coming to the library only during their study hall periods--and even then only once a week because of inadequate library seating or for disciplinary reasons--their opportunity for borrowing materials is limited. Thus circulation statistics are affected. Circulation figures which are kept accurately, carefully, and consistently can be valuable as one means of evaluation of the library program.

The expert cataloging of library materials and practical circulation procedures for their use can help to make the library a place to which teachers and students come, confident that they will be able to get what they want without frustration and disappointment.

Notes

1. Standards for School Library Programs, op. cit., p. 112.

2. M. Bernice Wiese and Catharine Whitehorn, Centralized Cataloging and Processing in the Baltimore Public Schools; Five Year Report, 1956-1961. (mimeo.) Chicago: Am. Assn. of School Librarians.

3. Ibid., p. 10-11.

4. Personal interview with Mrs. Mildred Breiland, Head Cataloger, Library Processing Center, Albuquerque, New Mexico, Public Schools, March 28, 1967.

5. Richard L. Darling, Streamlining for Service. (School Activities and the Library, 1965), American Library Association, 1965.

6. Agner N. Tysee, "Card Catalogs versus Printed Book Catalogs and the Library User," In Robert E. Kingery and Maurice F. Tauber, eds., Book Catalogs. Scarecrow Press, 1963, p. 55 ff.

7. Library Guide (plastic reference chart), Data-Guide, Inc., 40-07 149th Place, Flushing, New York. 11357

8. Esther J. Piercy, Commonsense Cataloging; a Manual for the Organization of Books and Other Materials in School and Small Public Libraries. Bronx, New York: The H. W. Wilson Co., 1965, Appendix VII.

9. Mary E. Crookston, Unit Costs in a Selected Group of High School Libraries. U.S. Government Printing Office, 1942.

10. Warren B. Hicks and Anne Mary Lowrey, "Preparation and Cataloging Time in School Libraries," School Library Association of California. Bulletin, XXX (May, 1959), pp. 7-10.

11. Sysdac Charging Machine, Bro-Dart Industries, Los Angeles, California. 90025

12. John Kager, 'Sysdac Charging Machine,' In "Mechanical Adaptations and Photocharging," Drexel Library Quarterly, III (July, 1965), p. 21.

13. Lloyd C. Bingham, "Deerfield's Spontaneous AV Inventory," Educational Screen and Audiovisual Guide, XLIV (February, 1964), p. 40.

Selected Readings

Technical Processes

Bildersee, Max U. "The IMC Counterpart," Educational Screen and Audiovisual Guide, XLV (April, 1966), 45-46.

Advocates that producers of audiovisual material supply cards with their products.

"Commerical Cataloging Service," Library Journal, XCI (October 15, 1966), 5133-5135.

Coulter, R. W. "How to Cut Red Tape in Processing Library Books," School Management, X (November, 1966), 99-100.

"Crisis or Cul-de-Sac?" Library Journal, XCI (October 15, 1966), 5129-5135.

Series of comments by various librarians on the subject cataloging of children's books.

Eaton, Thelma. Cataloging 500; the Principles of Book Description. North Egremont, Mass.: Shadow Hill Press, 1966.

A programmed course introducing the library science student to descriptive cataloging.

Graycar, Marie L. "A Survey of Vertical Files in California Public High School Libraries," California School Libraries, XXXVII (May, 1966), 26-27.

Hogan, Dan E. "Let Your School Library Catalog Cut across the Media," Library Journal, LXXXIX (December 15, 1964), 4981-4984.

Holdridge, R. E. "Cataloging nonbook Materials," Audiovisual Instruction, XII (April, 1967), 358-360.

Jackson, Sidney L. "Sears and LC Subject Headings: a Sample Comparison," Library Journal, LXXXVI (Feburary 15, 1961), 755-756+

Janecek, Blanche. "How to Treat a Paperback," School Libraries, XV (January, 1966), 28-29.

Jones, Milbrey L. "Technical Services in School Libraries; an Analysis of the Literature, 1951-61," Library Resources and Technical Services, VII (Spring, 1963), 189-196.

The same article appears in the October 1963 issue of School Libraries.

Kaiser, Walter H. "Synchronized Book Processing," Library Journal, LXXXVI (February 15, 1961), 752-754.

Use of Publisher's Weekly and Book Publishing Record for cataloging new books.

Lees, Gladys L. "Mechanization Moves into our Libraries," American School Board Journal, CLI (November, 1965), 28-29+

Perreault, Jean. "Computerized Cataloging: The Computerized Catalog at Florida Atlantic University," Library Resources and Technical Services, IX (Winter, 1965), 20-34.

Pressler, Joan. "Organizing Library-based A-V Materials," School Libraries, XIV (March, 1965), 43-47.

Rowland, Arthur Ray. "Cataloging and Classification in Junior College Libraries," Library Resources and Technical Services, VII (Summer, 1963), 254-258.

Williamson, Marion D. "Down with Dicta," [letter] Library Journal, XCI (November 15, 1966), 5666.

How a high school library found the lack of complete processing of paperbacks to be a handicap with regard to nonfiction.

Yessner, Bernice L. Administering a Filmstrip Collection. New York: McGraw-Hill, Inc., 1966.

Although this pamphlet chiefly describes the Library Filmstrip Center available for purchase from McGraw-Hill, it includes information of value to anyone processing filmstrips.

Centralized and Cooperative Processing

Carhart, Frances D. Southwest Missouri Library Services, Inc.: A Study in Co-operative Centralized Technical Services. Chicago: American Library Association, 1962.

Coburn, Louis. A Plan for Centralized Cataloging in the Elementary Schools of New York City. New York University, 1961. Library Science Ph.D. thesis. Available on microfilm from University Microfilms, Ann Arbor, Michigan. 48106

Darling, Richard L. "Is Central Processing for You?" Library Journal, XCI (December 15, 1966), 6153-6156.

Hendricks, Donald D. Comparative Costs of Book Processing in a Processing Center and in Five Individual Libraries... Springfield, Illinois: Illinois State Library, 1966.

Lightfoot, Robert M. "Can Cooperative Cataloging Work?" Library Journal, LXXXVI (February 15, 1961), 750-752.

Describes experiences of cooperative cataloging of microfilm copies of a Lincolniana collection by four university libraries. Advocates cooperative cataloging of specialized collections.

Lively, G. M. "Creative Elementary School Library and Centralized Processing," Wilson Library Bulletin, XXXVI (May, 1962), 753-757.

Moore, Everett L. "Processing Center for California Junior College Libraries--A Preliminary Study," Library Resources and Technical Services, IX (Summer, 1965), 303-317.

"Processing Centers; Guidelines for Study," School Libraries, XII (January, 1963), 40-41+

Sedgewick, Eleanor, "Centralized Cataloging Services in a Fast-growing School District; Fullerton Union High School District, California," Wilson Library Bulletin, XXXV (October, 1960), 148-150.

Commercial Cataloging

Frary, Mildred P., "Commercial Cataloging, Processing in the Los Angeles Schools," School Libraries, XV (January, 1966), pp. 11-15.

Westby, Barbara, "Commercial Cataloging Services: A Directory," Library Journal, LXXXIX (April 1, 1964), 1508-1518.

Book Catalogs

Harris, Ira, "Reader Services Aspects of Book Catalogs," Library Resources and Technical Services, VIII (Fall, 1964), 391-398.

Jones, Bob, "The Compact Book Catalog--by Photographic Process," Library Resources and Technical Processes, VIII (Fall, 1964), 366-369.

Manuals for Technical Processes

Chicago. Public Schools. Cataloging and Processing Procedures for Elementary School Libraries... Department of Library Science, Chicago Teachers College, 1959.

Dennis, Donald D. Simplifying Work in Small Public Libraries. Philadelphia: Drexel Institute of Technology, 1965.

Hopkinson, Shirley L. The Descriptive Cataloging of Library Materials. San Jose, Calif.: Claremont House, 1963.

Mary Annette, Sister. A Manual for Cataloging School Libraries, 3rd rev. ed. Sioux City, Iowa: Briar Cliff College, 1959.

Olson, Lowell E. Effective Book Processing; A Handbook for Librarians. Minneapolis, Minn.: Library Methods, 1960.

Westhuis, Judith Loveys. Cataloging Manual for Nonbook Materials in Learning Centers and School Libraries. Ann Arbor: Michigan Association of School Librarians, 1966.

Circulation

"Catholic High School Libraries Shelve and Circulate Paperbacks," Library Journal, LXXXIX (May 15, 1964), 2166.

Heinritz, Fred. "Circulation Procedures" [letter], Library Journal, XCI (November 15, 1966), 5666-5668.

Kirkwood, Leila H. Charging Systems. (The State of the Library Art, vol. 2, pt. 3) New Brunswick, New Jersey: Rutgers - The State University, 1961.

Ruecking, Frederick, Jr. "Selecting a circulation-control System: a Mathematical Approach," College and Research Libraries, XXV (September, 1964), 385-390.

Chapter VIII

Housing the School Library

In making plans for modern school library quarters, first consideration is given to the educational objectives of the school and its curriculum as they are related to library service in the library proper and throughout the school. Modern school libraries serve all areas of the school curriculum; they attempt to meet individual and group needs of both students and teachers; they aid in the guidance program as administered by counselors; they assist in carrying out extra-curricular activities. The library's contents are not limited to books, but incorporate all kinds of learning materials which are available for use in the best way possible. Thus the entire picture of the kind of service given by the library must be examined before making plans for its housing.

Quarters Prior to 1960

The days when the library was simply a place where students went to study from their textbooks are disappearing. For this kind of a library, which existed in many schools prior to 1960, plans called for one room about the size of two classrooms, with shelves attached to all available wall space. The room was apt to be located in one corner of the building, apart from classrooms, perhaps near the cafeteria, administrators' offices, or some other non-teaching area. The librarian or the teacher in charge spent much of his time checking attendance, issuing passes, reading announcements, and maintaining discipline. Although he hoped to give some reading guidance, little time was left for it. Administrators and teachers used to think of the library as a place to house books, largely recreational in nature, to be read in the students' spare time.

When a modern school system is planning a new school, practicing personnel in all phases of the school's program make up a committee to work with administrators and architects. Hence plans for the new school call for librarians to be included as members of the committee. Factors to be considered in making up the educational specifications for the library are: the purposes of the library and the services to be offered; location; physical requirements in relation to its services; people to be accommodated; kinds of space needed; furniture and equipment; provisions for sound control, lighting, heating and ventilation.[1] Some provision for all of these facilities is necessary even for the library in a small school of two or three hundred students, when the school has the concept of the library as necessary for excellence in teaching and learning.

Location

One of the first decisions to be made is the location of the library. Will it give best service when it is in one central location or when it is largely decentralized by department or subject? This decision depends on the size of the student body and the way in which the total program of the school is arranged.

Learning Resources Centers

For a school which has flexible scheduling where students are instructed in large groups together with small-group discussions, at least forty percent of the student's weekly schedule is spent in individual study. Trump says that this kind of study is best accomplished when all kinds of learning materials in each of several broad areas are brought together in one place.[2] Each of these learning resources centers consists of two areas, one for study and the other for work. In a science resources center, for example, is found many kinds of science books and magazines. Tape recordings, filmstrips, kits, and programmed learning materials are there, together with the recorders, viewers, and readers. All are available for use by individuals. The work area is a place where students work at various laboratory experiments. This learning resources center is thought of as a place where constant use is being made of the materials; students may be conferring with each other or with the teachers, librarians, and instructional assistants who are supervising the center. When such learning resources centers exist in a school, the central library contains specialized and very valuable materials and is used primarily by students with advanced or unusual projects.

Subject Libraries

A variation of Dr. Trump's proposal for decentralized library service is the establishment of study areas by broad subject, disconnected from laboratory or work areas. There are separate libraries for language and literature, social studies, the fine arts, science and mathematics, physical education, home economics, industrial arts, and business education. Depending on the size of the student body and the curriculum offerings, there are additions to these libraries or some are combined. Copies of certain frequently used reference works of a general nature are available in all of these subject libraries. A librarian who has a strong background in the subject, or a teacher with similar background who is a member of the library staff, is in charge. The central library contains a core collection of reference books as well as audiovisual materials and magazines that are of a general nature. In the central library is also found a collection of all kinds of books, recordings, and magazines of popular interest. The processing of all new materials is done here, unless materials are received already processed. Even in the latter case, there has to be a work room in the local library for mending books, filmstrips, etc., and for processing magazines, newspapers, and pamphlets. In addition to facilities for study, the central library incorporates browsing and listening areas. Librarians with a broad background of knowledge and who are particularly good at interpersonal relationships with teachers and students are in charge. When processing of new materials is done locally, librarians who have a particular ability in cataloging and in supervising other technical processes are needed here in the central library. A record of all library materials, regardless of where they are located in the school plant, is found here, while each subject library has a guide to its particular contents.

Separate Location for Print and Non-print Materials

Another possibility is to have all printed materials in one place in the school, and audiovisual media in another, separate location. When this is done, teachers and students tend to think of the former as the library and the latter as the audiovisual center. This separation encourages the idea that one kind of material is better, in itself, than another. It also makes it necessary for the person looking for information to go to two places; or to think in terms of only printed or only audiovisual material in relation to his need. On a large campus, one of the areas may not be used by some students or teachers simply because it is too far away.

An interesting variation of decentralized library service is found in the 1962 plans for the Ridgewood High School in Norridge, Illinois.[3] A central reading and study center is set up to contain largely books and magazines with provision for their use by individuals and small groups, together with an informal study area. Independent resource centers are planned for each subject area. Each center contains a study hall, a listening center, a viewing center, some books, a project area, and teachers' offices.

The Single Central Library

When a single library exists in a school plant, every effort must be made to locate it near the classrooms of subjects in connection with which students are likely to need the library most, i. e., social studies, English, and science. It should not be near places where there is constant traffic or considerable noise, and there must be possibilities for expansion. A single library provides all of the services available in the decentralized libraries, including a variety of materials, various kinds of physical facilities, and expert assistance. A complex of separate rooms is required for large and small group conferences, work areas for faculty and library staff, as well as places for individual study and browsing, plus areas for the materials themselves.

Advantages and Disadvantages of Central *vs* Decentralized Libraries

A school with decentralized libraries sees the chief advantage to be the easy and quick access to materials and expert assistance at a time when it is needed. To get to a single central library, particularly in a large school plant, may involve considerable time, tight restrictions as to when a student can go, and special passes. The advantages of single library quarters include less cost for duplication of some reference titles, of records of the library's contents, and of certain equipment. Expansion of one library is likely to be more easily arranged than in decentralized libraries.

Physical Requirements

Regardless of whether all materials and services are decentralized or are located in one library complex, consideration is given to the physical requirements for housing certain activities. To be described to the architects planning a new school library are those activities involving browsing and study by teachers and students, instruction in library techniques, reference work, viewing, listening, office space, work areas. Reading rooms should contain space for ten percent of the student body, allowing thirty to thirty-five square feet per student, according to AASL standards.[4] There should be one or more conference rooms at least 120 square feet in size for small group use. Separate rooms for viewing and for listening are needed. Work rooms for processing and mending of all kinds of library materials are necessary, their size and number depending on whether or not new materials are locally prepared and the extent of the size and nature of the collection. Reference books and back issues of magazines will require a separate area, and provision must be made for a browsing area. A room to accomodate an entire class is part of the library complex. The potential size of the total collection and where it is to be shelved and stored needs to be considered. When the library staff supervises the school's textbooks, they must be located near the library with plenty of space for the record-keeping and mending which are a large factor in their administration, as well as for their shelving.

Facilities for People

Among considerations concerning people to be accommodated are questions of the number of students to be seated in the reading rooms, the size and makeup of the library staff, special provisions for teachers. Each reading room should seat a maximum of eighty students.[5] A separate office is needed for one or more of the professional members of the library staff, and also for the library secretary. A workroom for clerical help is needed. Technicians who work with the audiovisual material may require a separate work area, depending on the size of this part of the library's collection in relation to the size of the collection of printed material. The potential growth of the library staff must be considered in planning work areas. Provision must be made in the library for a teachers' reading room which houses the professional collection. Just how many chairs and tables are needed here depends on the present and potential size of the faculty, as well as the kind of schedule each teacher has.

Equipment Needs

What amounts and kinds of equipment and furniture are needed? Shelving of various heights and depths is needed for books and magazines. The amount of shelving needed is based on eight books per shelf-foot for average size books and six books per shelf-foot for reference books.[6] Some of the shelving is used as dividers to separate reference area from browsing area, for example. Special cabinets and shelves are needed for filmstrips, film recordings, _Reader's Guides_, single maps, pictures, and pamphlets. Recommended basic audiovisual equipment for high schools includes the following:

16mm Sound Projector	1 per 10 teaching stations (classrooms)
8mm Projector	1 per building
2 x 2 Slide Projector	1 per building
Filmstrip or Combination Filmstrip-Slide Projector	1 per 10 teaching stations
Filmstrip Viewer	1 per 3 teaching stations
Overhead Projector (classroom type)	1 per 4 teaching stations
TV Receivers	1 per department where programs are available
Record Players	1 per 10 teaching stations
Tape Recorders	1 per 10 teaching stations

Other kinds of projectors are needed as well as other recorders.[7]

Furniture Needs

It is good to have both round and rectangular tables each seating four students, figuring five feet of space between the tables. Typical living room chairs and tables are needed for the browsing area. With today's emphasis on meeting the needs of each student, individual study tables or carrels are becoming more and more popular. A wide variety of ways exist in which carrels can be combined into groups of two or more. The carrels come in a variety of styles and materials. Some have panel dividers made of accoustical material, fiberboard, cork, or translucent plastic. Some carrels contain storage units, typing units, shelves for books, or equipment for plugging in recorders and viewers. "The learning laboratory station or carrel... is simply a place or environment designed especially for learning which may cluster a variety of media. It is an environment, incidentally, which according to studies now under way, may be influenced more significantly in effectiveness by its actual size, its relative isolation of one student from others, design of the control panel and so on, than by what it actually communicates through tapes, films, slides, etc."[8]

Special desks for the reference and circulation functions must be provided, as well as standard desks and shelves for the library offices. Workrooms require cabinets, sinks, repairing equipment and supplies of a special nature for work with printed and audiovisual materials.

Control of Sound, Heat, Ventilation, Light

Serious consideration is given to sound control, heating, ventilation, and lighting in the library. The use of carpeting can affect both the heating and the sound control, as well as being an important factor in the general atmosphere of the library. In libraries with large open areas, carpeting is particularly valuable in controlling sound. Air-conditioning with its constant background hum is also effective in masking sharp sounds which distract the library user. Accoustical treatment of ceilings and walls helps to mask the sound of typewriters, projectors, and recorders which exists in various parts of the library complex.

Extremes of temperature can create considerable discomfort for the library user. It can be controlled through the use of drapes, shades, shutters, exhaust vents and fans. Air conditioning is a necessity in some climates and it is advisable in others, because it allows for good mechanical control over the temperature.

The kind and location of windows obviously affects the light in the library. Although windows are good because they provide natural light, large ones which go from floor to ceiling usually result in glare so that they must be covered with drapes, blinds, or overhang. The following suggestions for lighting will aid in planning school libraries:

> Windows should permit a view of outside landscapes.
> Low windows may cause objectionable glare.
> Gray glass windows in reading rooms reduce glare and heat from the sun.
> Large ornamental type glass areas which admit too much bright light should be avoided.
> Light reflecting walls, ceilings, and furniture are recommended.
> Artificial lighting should be provided as though no other light sources were available.[9]

Designing and planning school library quarters is a complex business. The librarian-member of the committee must be able to work out the educational specifications, describing for the architect the library's activities, people to be accommodated, and kinds of areas needed, as well as the services offered. Not only the present needs but possible changes in the way of new kinds of materials and programs must be planned. No matter what ideas the librarian has in mind, they must be incorporated into the amount of space allowed for the library and the budget limitations.

Notes

1. Dwayne E. Gardner, "Educational Specifications for the School Library," _ALA Bulletin_, LVIII (February, 1964), 115.

2. J. Lloyd Trump, "Independent Study Centers: Their Relation to the Central Library," _National Association of Secondary School Principals Bulletin_, L (January, 1966), 45-51.

3. _Profiles of Significant Schools: High Schools 1962._ New York: Educational Facilities Laboratories, n.d., pp. 43-44.

4. _Standards for School Library Programs_, op. cit., p. 119.

5. _Ibid._

6. _A Yardstick for Planning School Libraries._ American Library Association, 1966, p. 2. (mimeographed)

7. _Quantitative Standards for Audiovisual Personnel, Equipment and Materials._ Washington, D.C.: Department of Audiovisual Instruc-

tion, National Education Association, 1966, pp. 11-13. (mimeographed)

8. C. Walter Stone, "Research and Practical Experiences of Recent Years that Support the Concept of the School Library Materials Center," In The School Library Materials Center... edited by Alice Lohrer. University of Illinois Graduate School of Library Science, November 3-6, 1963. Distributed by The Illini Union Bookstore, Champaign, Illinois.

9. James L. Taylor and others. Library Facilities for Elementary and Secondary Schools. (OE-15050) Washington, D. C.: U. S. Dept. of Health, Education, and Welfare, 1965. p. 36.

Selected Audiovisual Materials

* Planning a School Library. 16mm film; sound, color, 23 min. 1957. Remington Rand Division, Sperry Rand Corp.

Available on loan from district offices of Remington Rand.

* Remodeling the Elementary School Library. Filmstrip; 63 frames, color, Manual. 1961.

*Available on loan from Headquarters Library, American Library Association, for payment of round-trip shipping charges. In the case of films, there is also a three-dollar fee.

Selected Readings

American Library Association. Library Administration Division. Planning School Libraries: A Selected Bibliography. The Association, 1964. (mimeographed)

"Case Studies in School Library Planning," ALA Bulletin, LVIII (February, 1964), 116-122.

This issue of the Bulletin also includes: "What Happens in the School Library," "How the Architect Works," "What Next in School Libraries?" "A Short Bibliography on Planning School Library Quarters."

DeBernardis, Amo, and others. Planning Schools for New Media. Portland, Oregon, Division of Education, Portland State College in cooperation with the U. S. Office of Education, 1961. (pamphlet)

Ellsworth, Ralph E. and Hobart D. Wagener. The School Library: Facilities for Independent Study in the Secondary School, edited by Ruth Weinstock. Educational Facilities Laboratories, 477 Madison Ave., New York, 1963.

Johnson, Marvin R. A. "The High School Library--A Service and a Place," The High School Journal, L (November, 1966), 91-95.

Krohn, Mildred L. "Learning Center Experiment at Shaker Heights," School Libraries, XII (May, 1963), 27-30.

Library Building Institute. Problems in Planning Library Facilities... edited by William A. Katz and Roderick G. Swartz. American Library Association, 1964. "School Libraries," pp. 153-188.

Includes articles on the school library and the architect, the departmentalized school library. Also gives descriptions and plans of specific libraries.

Library Buildings and Equipment Institute. Planning Library Buildings for Service, edited by Harold L. Roth. American Library Association, 1964. "School Libraries," pp. 42-44; 116-127.

McJenkin, Virginia. "New Quarters for Fulton County School Library Services," School Libraries, XI (May, 1962), 11-16.

Messman, Howard A. Building Materials in Library Construction. (Occasional Papers No. 67) Urbana, Illinois: University of Illinois, Graduate School of Library Science, March 1963.

"Planning School Library Quarters," ALA Bulletin, LVIII (February, 1963), 103-128.

School Buildings Issue [annual] School Management, X (July, 1966) Articles include: "The Cost of Building Index," "Current Trends in School Facilities," "31 Solutions to your School Building Problems."

Tanzman, Jack. "How to Build around New Teaching Ideas," School Management, VII (December, 1963), 49-51+

Taylor, Kenneth I. "How to Plan and Equip an Instructional Materials Center," The Nation's Schools, LXVII (January, 1961), 53-60.

Chapter IX

School Library Personnel

The administration of the school library as a materials center requires many kinds of personnel, both for the local school and for state-wide assistance.

National Leaders

In their efforts to improve library programs, school librarians look for leadership and assistance at the national level. These national leaders are found in the United States Office of Education, professional organizations, and library education programs. Among those national leaders who are making outstanding contributions are: Eleanor Ahlers, University of Washington; Richard L. Darling, Director, Dept. of Instructional Materials, Montgomery Public Schools, Maryland; Rachel De Angelo, Drexel Institute; Lucile Hatch, University of Denver; Mary V. Gaver, Rutgers University, 1966-67 president of the American Library Association; Frances Henne, Columbia University; Frances Kennon Johnson, University of North Carolina, Greensboro; Alice Lohrer, University of Illinois; Jean E. Lowrie, Western Michigan University; Mary Helen Mahar, Library Services Branch, U. S. Office of Education; Peggy Sullivan, Knapp School Libraries Project; Carolyn Whitenak, Purdue University. As these national leaders take part in meetings, serve on committees and write for various publications, local school librarians can receive the benefit of their ideas.

State Leadership

Recognition of the significance of leadership on the state level is given both by the American Association of School Librarians through its _Standards for School Library Programs_ and by the Council of Chief State School Officers. In the latter's publication, _Responsibilities of State Departments of Education for School Library Services_, the following statement is made: "The state department of education should provide competent professional school library supervisory personnel sufficient in number to meet the needs of the state department's program of service to school libraries."[1]

Library personnel at the state level make important contributions to the improvement of school library programs. The number of states with school library supervisors has increased from twenty-six states with one or more supervisors in 1959 to thirty-six in 1963, and forty states in 1966. Throughout this book, the library has been thought of as including all kinds of materials for use in many services; hence, at the state level, all learning materials should be supervised by one person, whether he is called library specialist, instructional materials director or is given some other title. He may have various kinds of specialists working under his administration.

Local Supervisors

As school libraries increase in number and services, the need for a supervisor in the local school system becomes apparent. He is apt to work within the department of instructional services. He is a member of committees and serves as a consultant with many persons who have system-wide responsibilities in other areas. He keeps the superintendent and central office personnel informed on new developments in the library field.

The number of library supervisors and the amount of clerical or secretarial help needed by the supervisor depends on the size of the system, the existing library program, and any centralized services provided. The AASL standards recommend one supervisor for a system having five or more schools with enrollments of 200 or more students.[2] In urban centers it is obvious that one supervisor can do little except make a beginning in giving service. He needs assistants who may work only with elementary schools, or who may assist largely in the centralization of the selection and acquisition of materials.

An interesting division of responsibility for supervisory personnel is seen in the large Houston (Texas) Independent School District. Here there are three specialists who serve in parallel positions under the director of instructional materials services: the supervisor of library services, the assistant director of audiovisual education, and the supervisor of radio, TV, and film production.[3]

How Supervisors Help Local Schools

For the local school librarians, the supervisor gives assistance in planning new services, in-service education, system-wide meetings for the discussion and evaluation of materials and services. He encourages librarians to acquire further professional education. He initiates centralized ordering and processing where it does not exist, thus providing certain economies for the system. As he represents the system at national conferences and meetings, he reports to local librarians and other personnel concerning new ideas learned or projects discussed, particularly relating them to local needs. He serves as a member of the planning committee for new school plants and organizes the selection of a new library's basic collection. He interprets budget needs to the superintendent, as revealed through his close contacts with each library. One of the supervisor's major tasks is to interpret the role of the library to everyone with whom he comes in contact in the world of education, so that people are made aware of the importance of the library in all phases of the school program.

The need for school library supervisors was seen in the one thousand applications received by the six NDEA Institutes given in the summer of 1966 which were expressly offered for supervisors.

A 1967 Bowker publication, *School Library Supervisors Directory*, is a valuable guide to the 850 persons in state, county, district and city supervisory positions. The *Directory* also lists administrators of various federal funds for libraries and gives statistical information about the schools in the area in which the supervisors work.

Duties of the Local Library Staff

As we think of the good school library as one which incorporates the best possible selection, organization, housing, and use of all kinds of learning materials, the key to the service is the local library staff. The number and kind of personnel varies with the size of the school and the nature of the library collection. No school of 200 students can expect to have a strong library program without a full-time staff of one librarian and one clerk, even if there are very few audiovisual materials in the library. In a school of 900 students, there should be four librarians, one audiovisual technician, and three clerks. Depending on the extent and nature of the audiovisual program, specialists in materials production are needed. One of the librarians is designated as head librarian and supervises all library services. All of the librarians are given opportunities to work directly with teachers and students, rather than one spending all of his time in cataloging, another in selection, etc. When the technical processes are done in the local school, one librarian is in charge of them. Although he may do some of the work himself, he oversees work done by other professional and clerical members of the staff. For the complete processing of a single book, filmstrip, or recording, ten minutes of a librarian's time and twenty minutes of a clerk's time are needed.

Selection, cataloging, compiling bibliographies, and many other tasks are important jobs which directly affect the library program, and time must be given to them by all members of the staff. All of these services, however, are a means toward guiding teachers and students in the best use of the library. Therefore, most of the librarians' time should be spent with teachers and students. If the four librarians in a school of 900 spent all of their time in working with individual students, approximately six or seven minutes would be all that could be spent with each student.

Sub-Professional Personnel

School library services demand good help from employees with considerably less training than professional librarians. Many tasks in connection with acquisitions, cataloging, processing, circulation, publicity, and use of library materials need the qualifications of sub-professional personnel. These staff members known variously as library assistants, clerks, secretaries, and technicians need the qualities of accuracy, flexibility, patience, adaptability, and general intelligence. The training of these people to meet the needs of their work in libraries is often done "on the job," and some librarians think that this is the best kind of training. Assuming that a person applying for a position as library clerk, for example, has had specialized training in filing and record-keeping and appears to be generally intelligent and adaptable, the knowledge peculiar to libraries can be obtained in a program of on-the-job training after he is employed.

Training of Sub-Professional Personnel

However, there are special programs which exist for the training of sub-professional library personnel, particularly for those who want to work in school and public libraries. A surprising number of programs for library technicians is listed in American Junior Colleges. A survey of twenty-four such institutions offering courses for library clerks and technicians was made under a contract with the U. S. Office of Education by John L. Martinson in 1965.[4] Most of the programs had been established for less than five years; thirteen of them were in California; most had probably graduated twenty or more students in the preceding three years. They were established because of the need for sub-professional personnel in the local area. At the time of the survey, it was evident that these were on-going programs, with growth in enrollments and placement of graduates. The students were largely women who had been out of school for fifteen or more years; many of them were already working in libraries but wanted to upgrade their positions through further education. Others had become interested in library work through their own or their children's use of libraries. A growing number of recent high school graduates were students in these programs for library technicians.

Martinson describes eight case studies of programs for library technicians in his survey.[5] One of the strongest programs appears to be that of City College of San Francisco. With thirty-two students registered for the beginning course in the fall of 1965, it offers a sequence of courses leading to an Associate of Arts degree at the end of two years. At this college, in addition to courses in Library Technology, the emphasis is on liberal arts.

A different kind of program for sub-professionals described by Martinson is offered at Palomar College, San Marcos, California, where seventeen hours gives a certificate in library science. As well as straight library science courses and practical experience, this program includes business courses such as typewriting, filing, and general office procedures. The graduates are designated as library clerks rather than technicians.

Job Descriptions

As sub-professional positions are created and increased in school libraries, great care must be taken to compile detailed job descriptions of the work of each of the various positions, together with the level of responsibility and the educational and personal requirements. The position of technician is one of more responsibility than that of library clerk. Some technicians and clerks may work only with audiovisual material and others with printed material. On the other hand, the division may not be by type of material but by library department. Some personnel may work in the technical processes department where they assist in the acquisition and cataloging of books, pamphlets, filmstrips, records, and the ordering of films through a rental service. Others may work only in the circulation department. Regardless of how the sub-professional work is divided, a list of the duties of each position must be specified in order that employer and employee may see just where each job begins and ends. A committee of the American Library Association has prepared "a statement of the definitions of the sub-professional or technician class of library employees..." which should be of value here.[6]

Teachers on the Library Staff

The use of professional teachers as members of large school library staffs has been tried in some places. When large libraries include two or more subject-oriented learning centers in various locations throughout the school plant, professional teachers can function effectively as library staff members. At Roosevelt High School, Portland, Oregon, one teacher is assigned to the library for each period during the school day, and some teachers supervise the library during evening hours. The subject specialties of these teachers make them valuable assets to the library, and the teachers themselves gain a greater understanding of the full library program.

Shortage of Librarians

In spite of the fact that there are more than three hundred library science programs of various kinds in accredited institutions of higher education, there is a tremendous shortage of all kinds of librarians. The shortage of school librarians is especially critical. In 1964, there were 25,000 professional librarians who had fifteen or more hours of library science serving those public schools which had centralized libraries.[7] If AASL standards of one librarian for each group of three hundred students are met, 87,000 more school librarians are needed to staff the 56,000 centralized school libraries.

Commission on a National Plan for Library Education

The growing concern on the part of librarians for education in their profession culminated in 1962 with the establishment by the American Library Association of the Commission on a National Plan for Library Education. The complexity of the Commission's task is apparent when one thinks of the numerous aspects of education for librarianship. Among the oldest questions is the relationship between clerical and professional work. The nature of library work as it relates to the demand for information services and new methods of information storage and retrieval are also topics for frequent discussion. Although this writer takes the position that school librarians should administer all kinds of materials, there are some librarians who believe that the newer media should be supervised by some other agency in the school. In this connection, the Commission proposes that "attention be given to present and probable future personnel requirements of school, college, public, and special libraries; of educational and research agencies requiring specialized personnel for handling audio and visual media; and of agencies engaged in providing specialized technical and scientific information regardless of the means through which such information is required, organized, and disseminated, or the degree of analysis to which it is subjected."[8] The Commission has recommended that the American Library Association establish an office for research and experimentation in library education and personnel administration, with the following activities to be carried out in succession: a study of the characteristics of present-day librarianship, together with desirable philosophy and practice to meet the information needs of society; consideration of the present needs of library education as well as a study of the nature, content and techniques of professional education in other professions; the kind of action program needed to implement the foregoing, preceded by nationwide programs for improving the utilization of professional staff and updating in-service library personnel and library school faculties.[9]

Certification Requirements

School librarians must meet each state's educational requirements for teachers as well as for librarians. This often means more hours of education courses than of library science, thus implying that the librarian is first a teacher and second, a librarian. Whether or not librarians really need the same number and kind of college credits as teachers is debatable. Certainly some knowledge of educational principles, guidance, high school curriculum, and adolescent psychology is necessary for the librarian in the secondary school; however, when methods courses, statistics, and other education courses are required for librarians, the hours of credit in library science and the all-important subject knowledge are likely to be cut down. As suggested by Elinor C. Saltus, it may not be in the best interests of the school for administrators to be forced to employ as a librarian a certified teacher who has a few hours of library science.[10] Furthermore, the requirement of teacher certification for school librarians leaves no room for the employment of professional librarians who have been working with children or young people in public libraries. The entire picture of certification for school library personnel must be studied by professional groups.

The number of hours of library science needed for certification as secondary school librarians varies from state to state. However, the requirements set by regional accrediting agencies often influence the states. For example, in 1962 both the North Central Association of Colleges and Secondary Schools and five of its member states required fifteen hours of library science.[11] Many of the states in the Northwest Association follow the pattern of the Association in having graduated requirements based on enrollment.[12]

Whether library science education for school librarianship should be as extensive as that for positions in college, public, and special libraries is a problem which has been under considerable discussion in recent years. The attitude of the American Association of School Librarians toward this question is plainly stated: "The basic program of general and professional education for the school librarian is a five year program..."[13] The Association along with other professional groups does recognize that some positions can be filled by personnel with less education. The Knapp School Library Advisory Committee recommends that a person certified as a teacher with minimum certification as a school librarian should serve directly under a fully qualified librarian who is either the head librarian in a school or a supervisor in a district.[14]

Library Science Courses

What kind of library science courses are desirable for the prospective school librarian? The minimum of fifteen hours should include basic courses in the selection, organization, and guidance in the use of materials, as well as reference work and the role of the library in modern society. Head librarians and persons in supervisory positions need additional courses in administration, reading interests of young people, history of books and libraries, subject bibliography, and field or practice work. Assuming that these librarians have responsibility for all media, they need further knowledge of the selection, organization and use of audiovisual materials, particularly if it was not included in the basic courses previously listed.

The program for librarianship as proposed in 1962 at San Jose, California, State College was the result of revision of the California credential program. Under this legislation, librarians were included in each of the five-year programs of training for elementary, secondary, and junior college teachers. At San Jose State College, requirements for librarianship include forty-five units of general education, forty-five of an academic major, twenty-four in professional education, twenty-seven in librarianship, and thirteen units of electives. Thirty of the foregoing units are at the fifth year level. Among the courses in education and in librarianship, all of which are at the fourth and fifth year levels, are: American School System, Materials Preparation, The Learner, Curriculum and Methods, Administration of Materials Centers, School Library Administration, Technical Process, Basic Reference Materials, Book Selection for Children and Young Adults, Library and School Relationships, Selection of Special Materials, Practice Teaching, Library Field Work.[15]

Post-Master's Program

An interesting program is offered at the post-master's level at Western Michigan University for the position of Educational Specialist in Librarianship. In order to make up a total of thirty hours in addition to the required basic courses, a student can elect to take courses such as Introduction to Computer, Elementary School Library Materials, Field Assignment Seminar, Readings in Librarianship, History of Books and Printing, two Subject Bibliography courses, Government Publications, Curriculum Enrichment Materials, Libraries and Multi-Sensory Communication Media, Administration of the Instructional Materials Center, and Information Storage and Retrieval.

Undergraduate Programs of Library Science

A problem which it is hoped will be thoroughly studied by the National Commission on Library Education is the nature and content of the many undergraduate programs of library science and the graduate programs which are a part of colleges of education. Of the 319 programs in library science described in the *Library Education Directory 1964-65*, 301 offer specialization in school librarianship.[16] Of the programs offering one or more courses at the graduate level, thirty-four offered a master's degree program accredited by the American Library Association with eleven of these offering a doctoral program.[17] From 1964 through 1967, the ALA accredited the master's program of eight additional institutions. Although the American Library Association accredits only institutions offering programs leading toward the master's or doctor's degree, the Association does have a library education standard for undergraduate programs. This standard was met in 1964-65 by 69 percent of the programs. The accredited institutions, both on the undergraduate and the master's level, graduate people who are placed in all kinds of positions, some entailing a great deal of responsibility. Whether these librarians turn out to be more or less successful than those who are graduates of an ALA accredited program is not known. The question arises as to what extent those which meet no ALA standard approximate the training given for library technicians or at the other extreme approximate the education received in the accredited programs.

As school libraries continue to expand in numbers and services the need for professionally trained personnel will increase. The ALA accredited library schools are not producing all of the school librarians. Of the 2,586 known placements of people graduating from these schools in 1965, the majority were placed in college and university library positions.[18]

Entrance Requirements to Graduate Library Science Programs

Entrance requirements to graduate library science programs vary considerably. Some have no requirements other than the basic ones necessary for admission to the college or university itself. Those accredited by the American Library Association frequently require from six to twelve undergraduate credits in library science. Often these credits must be earned at their own university. When they have been acquired elsewhere, some of the ALA accredited schools ask that the students take a special examination covering the material, as a prerequisite for entrance to the graduate program. A third possibility is the acceptance of the undergraduate courses, provided they are from an institution accredited by its regional association. The University of Washington, for example, gives students credit for a minimum of twelve quarter hours of undergraduate library science courses acquired at any regionally accredited institution.[19]

Admission requirements other than credits in library science are typified by those of the University of Illinois Graduate School of Library Science: three letters of reference; personal interview with a member of the faculty or with an alumnus; in the prospective student's undergraduate program, a grade point average of at least 3.75 in the last sixty semester hours of study, an undergraduate major of at least twenty-four semester hours in almost any field (other than librarianship); sequences in science, social sciences, and humanities.[20] The formal educational requirements point up the importance of the need of librarians for a broad knowledge of many subjects as well as a major in one special field.

Commission on Professional Education of Media Specialists

Just as the American Library Association has a Commission for studying library education, so does the Department of Audiovisual

Instruction of the N. E. A. have a Commission on Professional Education of Media Specialists. A task force of this Commission which was appointed in 1965 met in the fall of 1966 to identify problems and the areas of concern, in order to carry out a study of education for media specialists. Just as the American Library Association realizes the lack of understanding that continues to exist about the duties of the librarian, the Department of Audiovisual Instruction (DAVI) is aware of the need to define the job of audiovisual specialist.

Even though DAVI in 1955 published a Directory of Graduate Programs for the Professional Education of Audio-Visual Supervisors, Directors, and Building Coordinators, the problem still exists, as Winman states, of "elevating audiovisual education from the level of a craft to the status of a profession."[21] In an attempt to discover what the content of professional programs for media specialists was, Winman made two studies. One was a study of forty-five selected university and college catalogs of graduate programs, in order to see if the existing programs could lead toward education for media specialists. The other involved sending a questionnaire to thirty-five well-known people in the educational media field to find out what courses they suggested should compose the professional preparation of a media specialist. As a result of these studies, the following conclusions were reached:

1) Professional preparation for media specialists must take an interdisciplinary approach.
2) Many institutions not offering such programs could do so within their present framework.
3) Media specialists are in fairly close agreement regarding the essential content of professional preparation.
4) Both theory and practice must be included in the program of education for media specialists.[22]

Certification of Media Specialists

Just as school librarians must be certified by state departments of education, so must media specialists. The Teacher Certification Board of Illinois in 1966 accepted reports concerning the certification of media specialists. One report dealt with the Standard

Special Certificate for Instructional Materials Specialization. This certificate is to be granted to people who combine preparation in library science and audiovisual instruction, as follows:

1) A minimum of 32 hours is required, with at least 40% of the courses being in audiovisual instruction, 40% in library science, and the remaining 20% in either or both fields; courses can be at either the graduate or undergraduate level.

2) Courses should be distributed over several subfields rather than a heavy concentration in any one field such as administration, cataloging, or the production of audiovisual materials; supporting courses should contribute to the development of the professional field of Instructional Materials.

3) Instructional Media specialists must also be certified as classroom teachers, although part of the student teaching may have been in the teaching of actual classes in the instructional program.[23]

It is plain to see that people preparing to work in modern school libraries, regardless of whether they are called librarians or instructional media specialists, need courses in the selection, organization, administration, and use of both print and audiovisual materials. It is hoped that the American Library Association and the National Education Association will continue to cooperate in every way to further their common goals as they relate to school library personnel.

Desirable Abilities

Hopefully the formal education for librarianship will develop those abilities needed by the librarian who administers the program in the local school. These abilities are prerequisites not only for the head librarian of a staff of other professional and sub-professional personnel, but also for the one who works as the only librarian in a school. He needs ability to develop good public relations in the school and in the community, so that library services performed and offered will be recognized for the real contribution which they make to the education of young people. In the local school, he must be able to assist with curriculum planning, so that as new courses are proposed he can knowledgeably interpret the role of the library in their development. As he administers the library itself, he needs ability in budget making and in management of the library's many basic processes and routines. Most of all he must be a planner and a seer--in order to view both the immediate and the long-range needs of the library as they pertain to services, personnel, materials, and physical facilities.

Image of the Librarian

The image of the librarian in the eyes of the public is slowly changing from that of a strict, unsmiling woman who maintains the library as if it were her personal property, to that of a friendly young man or woman who makes the library a place where everyone feels at home. Even today school librarians realize that the old concept still exists, as teachers make half-serious comments about keeping the books neatly on the shelves or about no talking in the library. Fogarty suggests that the lack of agreement within the library profession as to the librarian's function makes it difficult to get a true picture.[24] The history of librarianship reveals the emphasis on conserving books, while the modern emphasis is on service. School librarians must stop doing clerical tasks and other jobs which should be done by sub-professional personnel. They must spend most of their time working directly with teachers and students in individual and group service. When librarians themselves and other professional people in the schools see a library functioning as a service agency which welcomes all, the image of the librarian will change. Such a school library is administered by a librarian who uses automation and self-help whenever possible in the routine processes. In order to keep up with happenings in his own area, the librarian takes an active part in state and local organizations for librarians and teachers. As a member of national organizations, he has access to the latest developments and experiences in the school library field.[25] The librarian shows patience, consideration, and flexibility in his contacts with library users and potential users. Until school library staffs increase in number and kind of personnel, it may be difficult to erase entirely the old image of a school librarian.

Recruitment for school librarianship is a responsibility of

practicing librarians. As they make contacts with high school students and classroom teachers, they should search out those who appear to have the desirable characteristics and interests.

Student Assistants

The most obvious contacts for recruitment which school librarians have are the library's student assistants. As these students work daily in the library there are many opportunities for them to learn at first-hand about the profession. In some schools, student library assistants are paid an hourly wage for their work, and in others they receive academic credit. Only those who have previously worked for a year on a voluntary basis are apt to be paid, the money coming from the library's budget or fine fund. In 1963 and 1964, the Federal Neighborhood Youth Corps and the work-study program became sources of obtaining paid student help during the summer as well as the school year. Under these programs, high school students from low income families receive an hourly wage for working from ten to fifteen hours per week while they are attending school. Many other student assistants receive neither wages nor credit, as they are thought of as giving service to the school when they work in the school's various offices as well as in the library.

The student who works in the library has an opportunity to see new materials before they are ready to be circulated, to learn more about library materials and services, and to gain experience in filing, mending, making change, and record-keeping. From working in the library he may well acquire abilities basic to any future position he may hold: accuracy, neatness, promptness, initiative, personal responsibility, getting along with co-workers, pride in the organization of which he is a part.

Activities of clubs made up of library assistants give added opportunities for students to develop an interest in librarianship as a profession. As well as having meetings in which students acquire knowledge of local library needs and problems, these groups may visit public, college, and other libraries in the area.

At San Jose, California, High School, the AV Club consists largely of students who are assigned to the Instructional Materials

Center in order to learn how to be projectionists.[26] As well as receiving academic credit, the students feel a great deal of pride in being of service to their school. At the club meetings which take place during the school's activity period, time may be spent in discussing practical problems that have arisen or in learning how to operate a new piece of equipment. Familiarity with and knowledge of equipment is gained through the distribution of an equipment handbook. Occasional field trips are taken. These students are taught to be good projectionists as they learn to accept responsibility and to work quietly and quickly.

Meetings of all of the student library assistants in the system's high schools may be of value in the exchange of experiences or for interesting them in the profession of librarianship. State-wide library organizations for students exist in some states, notably those of Indiana and of Texas. For a number of years Indiana has had student assistant workshops during the summer at Indiana University. Among the activities of the Teen Age Library Association of Texas was the production in 1959 of the T. A. L. A. Activity Book and in 1961 of the T. A. L. A. Handbook.[27]

All too often the corps of student assistants is the only help which a librarian has. In many school libraries the staff depends on large numbers of volunteer student assistants to do the many routine tasks which would be better done by clerks. When as many as twenty-five or thirty students are needed each day to help in the library--four or five different ones during each class period and others before and after school hours--the problems of the library staff are likely to become great. The necessary on-the-job training is difficult to "sandwich in" between all of the other responsibilities of the library staff. A great deal of what is learned by a student today is forgotten by the time he appears for work tomorrow. When student assistants must maintain a certain scholastic rating in order to work in the library, there is bound to be some turnover at the end of each grade-report period, thus necessitating the training of new helpers. Situations where the great need for library help results in the exploitation of student assistants probably continue to exist in some schools. Student assistants must never be used as substitutes for paid clerks. When circumstances allow, however, their help can be of educational value and can foster a sense of service to the school. In addition, the possibility of encouraging some of them to enter the library profession should not be overlooked.

Up-dating Professional Education

Working librarians need to return to college for additional courses in order to up-date their training. Beginning in 1966, 900 full-time fellowships were made available through the United States Office of Education for experienced school personnel, including librarians. Among the more recent means of assistance for the education of librarians was the awarding in 1966 of 139 graduate fellowships in library and information science under the Higher Education Act of 1965.[28] More than 500 similar fellowships were made available in 1967. One of the National Education Association's Hilda Maehling Fellowships was awarded in 1967 to a junior high school librarian for the purpose of "producing self-instruction films on how to operate audiovisual equipment and on routine matters concerning the use of the library."[29] The NDEA Institutes for school librarians and for media specialists held during the summers of 1965, 1966, and 1967 were of great help in the education of both beginning and experienced school librarians. The American Library Association has produced a booklet, frequently updated, describing the many scholarships, fellowships, and loan funds available from library associations, state departments of education, and other sources. Many brochures concerning the various kinds of librarianship are also available from the ALA.

The whole picture of library personnel for the local school needs to be frequently examined in relation to the kind of work done and present and future plans. As physical facilities are enlarged or decentralization is contemplated, the effect of these changes on staff needs must be taken into account. Every few years, a study should be made to see to it that professional members of the staff are spending most of their time in the all-important guidance service.

As school enrollments increase, more staff members need to be added. Every effort must be made to maintain the standard of one librarian for every 300 students, with an additional half-time librarian when the library administers the total instructional materials program. The same number of clerks is needed for every 300-600 students in a full program of library service. Job descriptions for all library personnel may need to be re-examined.

Without an adequate library staff which has resourcefulness and imagination to carry out today's tasks and to plan for the future, the school's library will offer considerably less than the dynamic program needed to fill the demands of our schools.

Notes

1. Responsibilities of... op. cit., p. 9.

2. American Association of School Librarians. Standards... op. cit., p. 42.

3. Elenora Alexander, "The IMS Merger," Library Journal, LXXXIX (October 15, 1966), 4108.

4. John L. Martinson, Vocation Training for Library Technicians: A Survey of Experience to Date. Washington, D. C.: Communications Service Corporation, 1965.

5. Ibid.

6. Dorothy F. Deininger, Chairman. Report of Joint ad hoc Committee... on Sub-Professional or Technician Class of Library Employees. (mimeographed)

7. Mary Helen Mahar, "Inventory of Library Needs - School Libraries," In National Inventory of Library Needs, American Library Association, 1965, pp. 26-27.

8. "A Report from the Commission on a National Plan for Library Education," ALA Bulletin, LXI (April, 1967), 420.

9. Ibid., pp. 421-422.

10. Elinor C. Saltus, "Teacher or Librarian?" Library Journal, LXXXVII (December 15, 1962), 12-13.

11. Darling, Survey..., op. cit., p. 10.

12. Ibid.

13. American Association of School Librarians, Standards... op. cit., p. 60.

14. "The Knapp School Libraries Project is a Five-Year Demonstration Project," American Library Association, 1966. (leaflet)

15. Leslie H. Janke, "The Library Education Program of San Jose State College," In The School Library as a Materials Center... Proceedings of a Conference... May 16, 17, 18, 1962... U.S. Department of Health, Education and Welfare, 1963, pp. 63-68.

16. Sarah R. Reed and Willie P. Toye, Library Education Directory 1964-65, Washington, D.C.: U.S. Department of Health, Education, and Welfare, p. 5.

17. Ibid., p. 6 ff.

18. Donald E. Strout and Ruth B. Strout, "The Placement Situation 1965..." Library Journal, XCI (June 15, 1966), 3117-3126.

19. "Librarianship; University of Washington," Library News Bulletin [Washington State Library] XXXII (July-Sept., 1965), 195-196.

20. Herbert Goldhor, "From the Director's Desk," University of Illinois Library School Association. News Letter. Bulletin No. 79, Fall 1966, 11-12.

21. Raymond V. Winman, "An Interdisciplinary Approach to Planning a Program of Professional Preparation for Media Specialists," Audiovisual Instruction, XII (February, 1967), 110.

22. Ibid., p. 113.

23. Maurice Iverson and others, "Certification of Media Specialists: Illinois, New York, and Wisconsin," Audiovisual Instruction, XII (February, 1967), 117-119.

24. Dora F. Walker, "The School Librarian Builds a Public Image," Library Journal, LXXXVIII (September 15, 1963), 3258-3260.

25. See Appendix V for names and addresses of professional organizations.

26. Mildred V. Chatton, "An Important Aid to Teachers," Scholastic Teacher, LXXXVII (February 14, 1966), Suppl. 22-23.

27. The latter is available from Mrs. Luella Higley, Consultant in Library Services, Ft. Worth Schools, Ft. Worth, Texas. 76101

28. "Library Education Report," Journal of Education for Librarianship, VII (Winter, 1967), 196.

29. "Recipient of Classroom Teacher World Affairs Fellowship," NEA Reporter, VI (April 21, 1967), 2.

Selected Audiovisual Materials

Cooperating with the Librarian. Filmstrip; 37 frames, color, 1961. Essential Education, Box 968, Huntsville, Texas. 77340

Shows what librarians do. Good for training student assistants.

* Key to a Future. 16mm film; 15 1/2 min., color, sound, 1964. Massachusetts National Library Week Film Committee. Available from Wing Productions, 252 Great Road, Bedford, Massachusetts. 01730

Recruitment film, directed toward the high school student.

The Librarian as Media Manager. Tape; 26 min., 3 3/4 ips. Charles Burke, Box 494, Westport, Connecticut. 06880

* The Library and the Librarian. Filmstrip; 47 frames, color, 1961. Eye Gate House, Inc., 146-01 Archer Ave., Jamaica, New York. 11435

* Available on loan for payment of round-trip shipping charges from Headquarters Library, American Library Association, 50 East Huron St., Chicago, Illinois. 60611. In the case of films, there is also a three-dollar fee.

Selected Readings

Need for Librarians

Asheim, Lester. "Manpower: A Call for Action," Library Journal, XCII (May 1, 1967), 1795-1797.

First in a group of articles on "The Manpower Shortage."

Boas, Martha T. "More than Deliberate Speed," ALA Bulletin, LX (March, 1966), 286-288.

"Some reflections on the relation between manpower and educational needs in today's library world."

Gaver, Mary V. "Crisis in School Library Manpower - Myth or Reality?" (School Activities and the Library 1967) American Library Association. (pamphlet)

Lowrie, Jean E. "Personnel Needs for Today and Tomorrow," American School Board Journal, CLIII (December, 1966), 26-27.

Supervisors

Darling, Richard L. "School Library Supervisors: What They Do,"

School Libraries, XII (March, 1963), 31-33+

Hardin, Maurine S. "School Library Consultant Services, a California Achievement," School Libraries, IX (January, 1960), 29-30.

Mahar, Mary Helen, editor. School Library Supervision in Large Cities: Proceedings of a Conference... September 23, 24, 25, 1964. U. S. Government Printing Office, 1966.

The School Librarian: His Functions, Duties, Personal Characteristics

Anderson, Dorothy. "What's so Lively about the Career of a School Librarian," Illinois Libraries, XLVII (April, 1965), 298-300.

"A Composite Picture of the School Librarian," California School Libraries, XXXV (November, 1963), 5-10.

Results of a survey of secondary school librarians in Santa Clara County, California. Good picture of typical librarian's activities; also describes the library's contents, the budget, physical facilities.

Crawford, Lura. "Functional Staff for the High School Library," School Libraries, XV (March, 1966), 27-33.

Describes the work of the staff of the Oak Park and River Forest (Illinois) High School, one of the Knapp Project schools, serving over 3,300 students.

Edwards, Margaret A. "Pushing the Book," Library Journal, XCI (December 15, 1966), 6166-6168.

A plea for librarians to read books as well as to process them; fine picture of the kind of person a librarian working with teenagers should be.

Georgi, Charlotte. "This Librarian's Credo," Special Libraries, LVII (May-June, 1966), 305-307.

Library Manpower: Occupational Characteristics of Public and School Librarians, by Henry T. Dennan and Richard L. Darling. (OE 15061) Washington, D. C.: Government Printing Office, 1966.

Logsdon, James D. Achieving Quality in School Programs: The Leadership Role of School Librarians. School Library Development Project, AASL, 1961. (mimeographed)

Lunn, Mervel S. "What is a Successful Media Director?" Audio-visual Instruction, XII (February, 1967), 140-142.

Preston, Ellinor G. "The Librarian Sees his Role in the Materials

Center," Educational Leadership, XXI (January, 1964), 214-216.

Swarthout, Sherwin. "Professional or Paraprofessional?" Audiovisual Instruction, XII (February, 1967), 126-131.

Attempts to distinguish between the characteristics and functions of the various people working in the media field.

Taylor, Kenneth I. "Competencies Needed by School Librarians for Planning Quarters and Administering the Use of Materials Centers," In The School Library as a Materials Center... Proceedings of a Conference... May 16, 17, 18, 1962... U.S. Government Printing Office, 1963.

Wheeler, Helen. "27 Tips for the New Librarian," Library Journal, XCI (December 15, 1966), 6164-6165.

Wyman, Raymond. "The Instructional Materials Center: Whose Empire?" Audiovisual Instruction, XII (February, 1967), 114-116.

Education for Librarianship

Beringhausen, David K., ed. Proceedings of an Institute on Undergraduate Library Education: Standards, Accreditation, Articulation... Minneapolis, University of Minnesota, 1959.

Good, William J. "The Librarian: From Occupation to Profession?" Library Quarterly, XXXI (October, 1961), 306-320.

Hartz, Frederick R. and Eugene A. Pringle, "Education for Instructional Materials Centers," Drexel Library Quarterly, II (April, 1966), 172.

Inoue, Kyoko. "I Studied Librarianship," California School Libraries, XXXV (May, 1964), 28-30+

"Library Education and the Shortage: A Symposium," Library Journal, XCI (October 15, 1966), 4881-4898.

"Library Education and the Talent Shortage," [symposium] Library Journal, XCI (April 1, 1966), 1761-1773.

Lowrie, Jean E. "Education and Training of School Librarians," National Association of Secondary-School Principals Bulletin, L (January, 1966), 64-69.

McJenkin, Virginia, "Continuing Education for School Librarians," ALA Bulletin, LXI (March, 1967), 272-275.

"Professional Education of the Media Specialist," AV Communication Review, XIV (Summer, 1966), 185-201.

Sellers, Rose Z. "A Different Drummer: Thoughts on Library Education," Journal of Education for Librarianship, VI (Winter, 1966), 151-166.

Stone, Walter C., ed. The Professional Education of Media Service Personnel. Pittsburgh, Pennsylvania: University of Pittsburgh, 1964.

White, Carl M. The Origins of the American Library School. New York: The Scarecrow Press, Inc., 1961.

Sub-Professional Personnel and Their Duties

Annan, Gertrude L., "Library Technicians: Need, Training, Potentential," Medical Library Association. Bulletin, LII (January, 1964), 72-80.

Ersted, Ruth M. comp. Some Non-Professional Jobs in the School Library. School Library Development Project, American Association of School Librarians, 1962. (mimeographed)

Kolb, Audrey. "Library Technicians," Library News Bulletin [Washington State Library] XXXIII (October-December, 1966), 288-289.

McCurley, Paul. "The Move Forward: Courses for Library Technicians," Library News Bulletin [Washington State Library] XXXIII (October-December, 1966), 284-287.

Miller, Elwood E. "Proposed: A Media Clerk-Technician," Audiovisual Instruction, IX (November, 1964), 606-607.

Winnick, Pauline. "Work Opportunities in Public Libraries," In Two Blocks Apart [kit] Papers from an Institute sponsored by the Young Adults Services Division, American Library Association, July, 1966. (mimeographed)

List of 41 non-professional duties to be learned through on-the-job training.

Student Assistants

Benezra, Barbara and Elizabeth Goodman. "Helpers or Headaches?" School Libraries, XIII (March, 1964), 23-25.

Good ideas for using student assistants in the elementary school library.

Consear, Helen S. "Low-IQ Page Volunteers," Library Journal, LXXXIX (April 15, 1964), 1831+

Describes an experimental program in which 9th graders from a school's occupational education class were trained to work as public library pages.

Douglas, Mary Peacock. The Pupil Assistant in the School Library. Chicago: American Library Association, 1957.

McLaughlin, Ruth A. "The Kantagna Assistants," School Activities, XXXVII (February, 1966), 10-11.

A day in the life of a new student library assistant.

Student Library Assistants. [Selected references] Chicago: American Association of School Librarians, 1966. (mimeographed)

A good bibliography of books, pamphlets, magazine articles, and student guides.

Willett, Brother Franciscus, comp. Student Library Assistants, a Manual for Librarians. National Catholic Student Library Assistants Association, 1960. (pamphlet)

Wright, Alice E. "Pages and Student Assistants: Their Training and Care," Wilson Library Bulletin, XXXVI (May, 1962), 739-749.

Practical, detailed account of selection, recruitment, orientation, and training. Includes sample job description for a library page. Available as a reprint from the H. W. Wilson Company.

Chapter X

The Role of Principals and Other Administrators in the School Library Program

Much of the success or failure of the library program rests with the superintendent of schools and the principal of the local school. When the superintendent is concerned with the development of strong libraries, it is because he knows how significant they are in the maintenance of quality education. He is the one who leads the way in establishing policies for assuring effective library service. The library-minded superintendent influences the public in backing good school libraries; and as he works with the school board, he is able to get strong financial support from that body.

One way in which the superintendent makes known his concern for libraries is through his annual report to the board of education. A good illustration of such a report is the one made in 1966 by Robert L. Chisholm, superintendent of the public schools of Albuquerque, New Mexico. Here concern is expressed for the local need for more personnel to administer the complexities of a library in a world containing a vast array of constantly expanding knowledge. He also speaks of the future school library as a place which will contain knowledge not only in the form of books but also in films, tapes, diagrams, maps, and other materials. Librarians will be experts in developing packages of resources to meet the particular needs of each teacher. In addition to having its own wide collection, Dr. Chisholm sees the school library as having access to a central computer and to central information banks. This is an example of a superintendent expressing to a board of education his understanding of the significance of the school library in the total educational program.

Again, the leadership of the school system's superintendent in recognizing the importance of libraries is revealed in the history of the school system of Provo, Utah.[1] When Dr. J. C. Moffitt became superintendent of schools in 1937 he felt that one of the two chief characteristics of a good school was excellence in the library program. During more than twenty-five years in this position and with the full approval of the school board, Dr. Moffitt led the way in improving existing collections, centralizing libraries in old plants, and including central libraries in all new schools.

Where there is little or no school library service, the knowledgeable superintendent is apt to be the one who instigates setting up a "model" library or a "pilot" program of expanding service. In such a situation national standards for physical facilities, materials, and personnel are met as nearly as possible. Then a broad and flexible program of activities is put into action; provisions are made for principals, teachers, and others to see the program in action. Studies are made to see what kind of impression excellent library service makes on the program of the entire school.

The superintendent sees the need for supervisory personnel on a system-wide level, including that of the library. Some of these positions are in various subject fields, such as music, science, English, social studies, business education, and language. Other supervisory positions cut across subject fields including those in health, guidance and library service. The superintendent recognizes that library supervisors who have high quality professional education and considerable experience are able to do much to help clarify objectives, promote the wise expenditure of money, and improve library service in the local schools. As supervisors observe the functioning of libraries, they are the ones who report to the superintendent the need for better library quarters, for more materials or personnel. Library supervisors work closely with subject supervisors in assisting the local school to plan in-service training of teachers.

Although the effect of the superintendent's knowledge and influence can be great, the local library situation is directly influenced largely by the principal. The principal has some knowledge concerning all phases of the school's program. Just how much he knows about the library as well as his attitude toward it depends on his background of education and experience. If his knowledge is limited to that obtained in college and graduate school courses for administrators, it may be minimal or non-existent. His ignorance may be appalling, and his attitude may be, "I could not care less!" However, principals who have had personally satisfying experiences in libraries and whose families have benefited from library usage will have a positive attitude toward the school library and its staff. As principals attend conferences, visit other schools, and read in their professional journals about library service, they become more aware of the influence which a strong library can have on the entire school program.

The principal must recognize librarians as full members of the faculty since their background of education is comparable to that of other professional school personnel. Then he can depend on the librarians to keep him informed concerning new developments in library facilities, materials, and services. The head librarian who does not take on this responsibility fails in a very important obligation. It is his duty to be familiar with new developments not only for his own enlightenment but in order to interpret them to the principal, in relation to the local library situation.

No matter how strongly the library staff feels about the importance of its services, it cannot get very far in its program without the full cooperation and backing of the principal. Therefore, close communication between them must exist. Regardless of how the principal gains his understanding and appreciation of library programs, it is he who leads the way in supporting the library. Whenever changes in library procedures have been decided on, it is the principal who has the responsibility along with the library staff of lending active support. For a number of years, each teacher in a school may have been allotted a sum of money for the purchase of library books which she keeps in her room. When the decision is made to gather all of these books into a central library, the principal must do all that he can to see to it that teachers give up what they may consider to be "their" books. Furthermore, he must be able to explain to the teachers just what the values are of centralization of library materials. Schools which for years have had libraries sponsored by volunteers or run by a full-time teacher may not see why they are about to have the "luxury" of a professional librarian.

Again, the principal needs to know what the advantages are and be able to explain them to his teachers.

The librarian who has creative ideas and who makes plans for the future growth of the library in relation to the needs of the school's curriculum and students gains the confidence of the principal. Without that confidence, little will be accomplished.

A fine relationship can exist between librarians and counselors as they work together for the growth and development of each student. As counselors work with students, numerous needs which may be met through library materials are revealed. In the area of personal problems, the library staff can provide materials to meet specific needs. Problems in connection with study habits or particular courses which a student is taking can be alleviated through the use of library materials. The library staff must be alert to observe the needs of students for conferences with counselors. As students discuss their post-high school education and their vocational plans with counselors, the library is able to supply up-to-date information in these areas. The library staff and the guidance department can sponsor jointly a series of films on careers. At the beginning of each school year as the guidance department makes plans for the orientation of new students, the library staff should assist in every way possible. When counselors arrange for conferences with parents, library staff members as well as teachers may be able to contribute to the conference. Counselors can be of help to librarians as they assist in the selection of student assistants.

The abilities which the head librarian may or may not have in administering the total library program reveal themselves very readily in his relationships with principals, counselors, and other administrative personnel. Whether or not the service given by librarians is recognized by their fellow administrators as an important and necessary part of the school may well depend on the ability of librarians to communicate with administrators.

Notes

1. Shirley B. Pasman, "Board Motivates Local Library Program," American School Board Journal, CLI (November, 1965), 38-41.

Selected Audiovisual Materials

The Principal and the Librarian. Tape; 17 min., 3 3/4 ips. Charles Burke, Box 494, Westport, Connecticut. 06880

Selected Readings

Christine, Emma Ruth. "Listen to the Librarian!" California School Libraries, XXXVI (May, 1965), 19-21.

Plea for recognition by administrators and teachers of the librarian as a qualified teacher who has special competencies.

Derthick, Lawrence G. "You and the Administrator," Library Journal, LXXXVII (November 15, 1962), 4233-4235.

Elseroad, Homer O. "The Superintendent's Key Role in Improving School Libraries," National Association of Secondary School Principals, Bulletin, L (January, 1966), 1-5.

Gibbs, Wesley F. "The School Library - An Administrator Speaks," (School Activities and the Library 1966) Chicago: American Library Association. (pamphlet)

Haebich, Kathryn A. "Librarians and Counselors Together," Illinois Libraries, XLVII (December, 1965), 834-836.

Librarians and Counselors Work Together for an Effective Guidance Program in the School. Chicago: American Association of School Librarians, 1964. (pamphlet)

Schwilck, Gene L. "The Library Needs the Principal," National Association of Secondary-School Principals, Bulletin, L (January, 1966), 6-9.

Chapter XI

The Future: A Forecast of Things to Come

In looking toward the future, what are the developments which can be expected in the realm of school libraries? Since the library program cannot exist apart from the school program, let us look first at the possibilities for the high school of the future.

Within the next fifteen or twenty years, it is quite possible that the population of the United States will have risen to 249,000,000, an increase of seventy-one percent over the 1960 census. Of this number, as many as 125,000,000 may be in school. If people continue moving to urban areas, the bulk of the school age population may be located in 150 or 200 metropolitan centers. Thus schools will be much larger than they now are, suggesting the need for new administrative patterns, for more campus-style plants, and for a different pattern from the single central library. Regional planning in many areas, including library services, will probably take place as a result of the concentration of population in urban centers.

High Schools of the Future

In a speech at the 1965 convention of the National Association of Secondary School Principals, Harold C. Hunt of Harvard University pointed up five areas in which the secondary school fifty years hence may be different from what it is today.[1] In the first place, schools may be in clusters, each cluster serving as many as 20,000 children. Secondly, there will be greater financial support from the federal government and continued effort toward the equalization of educational opportunity. Along with this will come assessment on a national level of how much is being learned by various age groups in different parts of the country. The third prediction is that the school curriculum will be very much broader than it now is, with innovations being the accepted thing. In the fourth place, principals and teachers will have many kinds of specialists to help them. People to manage health, building, transportation, and food services will give principals more time to work directly with school personnel and with curriculum. Teachers will have the assistance of specialists in community resources, preparation of materials, and diagnostic evaluations. The fifth prediction concerns the many new pressures on school principals which will arise because of the greater size of schools and the speed of communication. Dr. Hunt sees great challenge for school personnel in the influence of "mass culture" whereby individual students requiring unique treatment may be lost and students are seen as groups to be manipulated. In the light of these predictions for schools of the future, let us look at their possible effect on the school library.

Role of the Federal Government

If the Federal government plays a larger role in the development of the school library, we may see further appropriations for all kinds of learning materials and equipment, for housing, and for education and employment of various kinds of professional personnel. Priorities will likely be given to those proposals which demonstrate originality in planning and to projects which are based on evidence of some effort already having been made by the local school. Appropriations may be available for more projects which are cooperative efforts of schools with other groups, such as those now available through Title III of the Elementary and Secondary Education Act of 1965.[2] As efforts to provide quality education for all children and young people continue, experiments with new methods of teaching and new kinds of materials may be financed in part through Federal funds. The library, naturally, will be directly involved in such experiments.

Efforts to assist the economically and culturally deprived segments of the population will doubtless continue to expand. Federal appropriations for school children who fall into these groups will include money for library materials and for paying for student help. Independent, non-profit organizations may well expand their assistance to Federal organizations working with deprived groups. Some of these will directly or indirectly affect the school library. For example, the

Fund for the Advancement of Education gave $300,000 in 1966 for projects to encourage leisure reading by deprived groups. The National Book Committee has worked with Community Action programs in the expansion of library services as a part of neighborhood centers in slums. The Fund for the Advancement of Education and the National Book Committee have jointly sponsored a program for supplying portable libraries for workers in Volunteers in Service to America (VISTA).

Library Materials

What will be the problems of the future in regard to the library's materials? With the explosion of knowledge, hundreds of new books and other materials are constantly appearing, and are likely to continue in large numbers. Therefore, the problem of expert selection becomes a major one for the school library staff. As more and more money for library materials becomes available from Federal sources, there may well be a temptation to relax principles of selection and to "take a chance" by ordering items which one would not choose, if the budget were more limited.

As well as continuing to rely on the well-known, established aids for printed materials, new ones will doubtless appear. The most recent source of reviews of selected paperbacks of interest to the school librarian is the quarterly publication, Kliatt Paperback Book Guide. Beginning in the spring of 1967, this service gives subscribers bibliographical information and brief annotations in the form of both loose-leaf sheets and cards.

It is hoped that the badly needed tools for selecting audiovisual materials will be available in the near future. The current plan to include reviews of non-print materials in each issue of the well-known Booklist and Subscription Books Bulletin will be of great help. The National Information Center for Educational Media has announced the publication of its Index to 16mm Educational Motion Pictures.[3] Planned as the first in a series of educational media tools, it gives comprehensive information, provided by the producers, on motion pictures currently available. Financed by a four-year grant from Mc Graw-Hill, NICEM actually combines the automated cataloging project of the University of Southern California with the Educational Media Index. It has as its main purpose to catalog, in a central computerized memory bank, data on all forms of audiovisual material.[4] The indexes to be produced by NICEM, while not serving as selection tools, will be of assistance to librarians in the same ways that are Books in Print and Subject Guide to Books in Print.

To help in the selection of materials, more cooperative reviewing groups will be organized. These may be composed of all the librarians of one school system or a combined group from two or more systems. The school and public librarians in a community could well work together in reviewing new materials for young people.

Books will continue to be a major part of the library collection. As collections grow larger, there may well be a greater need for more copies of certain books as well as a greater diversity of titles. Paperbacks will probably be used in even more ways than they now are. In addition to new titles, certain books long out of print will continue to reappear in paperback form. Giving paperbacks to students will be further explored, not only for the economically deprived but for all students.

The efforts being made in behalf of the deprived segments of the school population make for interesting possibilities in the writing and publishing fields. Perhaps in the future there will be more publications of books like the ones developed by the Board of Education of the City of New York and published by Silver Burdett Co. These four books contain short biographies of people from minority groups who made something of themselves.

When the uses of facsimile literature are more thoroughly explored, it may appear to a greater extent than it now does. "The March of America," consisting of one hundred titles varying from Columbus' report of his first voyage to Frederick Jackson Turner's famous essay on the Westward Movement, is a fine example of facsimile literature now available.[5]

Probably the greatest change in kinds of materials in the school library of the future will be in the addition of more audiovisual media. In the realm of film, 8mm is likely to be greatly expanded. Since it is particularly good for use with small groups and for individual instruction, it has great potentialities particularly for those schools which have flexible scheduling with large and small group teaching. The 8mm cartridge film and the small projector take up comparatively little storage room. They are easily operated and can be focused on any light surface.

A recent development in the motion picture field gives an idea of what the future may hold. A device for showing forty different sound motion pictures without changing reels has been produced. Its operation is similar to that of a juke box.

New tape recordings will be produced as well as different recording units for their use. Revere's stereo recording unit which can play for sixteen hours is one of the newer developments.[6] The future may see more cooperation among libraries which already have collections of educational tapes or which plan to specialize in this medium. An effort is currently underway to find out just what services can be given by those libraries now containing approximately 10,000 tape recordings, in cooperation with the National Tape Repository at the University of Colorado.[7] The possibility of making a union catalog of these tapes is one of the considerations.

The flexibility of transparencies, ease of use and storage, makes them one of the most popular of the new media products. Many more doubtless will be available in the future.

Television will be used more than it is today, both through the establishment of additional educational television channels and through the use of closed circuit television in local schools. The Television Information Office of the National Association of Broadcasters serves as an information outlet between the television industry and the public.[8] Educators will find its research studies and publications helpful. With the establishment in 1966 of the National Center for School and College Television at Indiana University, assistance can be expected in the location and distribution of effective television materials for classroom use.

Probably the production of multi-media resources will be one of the greatest future developments of materials for school libraries. Communication Films has produced a variety of such kits on various countries.[9] These kits contain study prints, filmstrips, records, and a variety of realia. Also, the audio-lingual textbooks of the Encyclopaedia Britannica Press which have teaching machines and filmstrips as well as texts are an interesting use of the multi-media approach to learning.

In the very attraction of the unusualness of some audiovisual materials together with their wealth and variety, it may be easy for the school library to "go overboard" in acquiring them and to neglect to select from the many new books. The school librarian of the future may well need "a renewed conviction that books are educators."[10] When we stop to think of the many advantages which books have over non-print materials, it will be impossible to neglect acquiring them.

Organization

What are the possibilities for the future organization of the school library? Technical processes including ordering, cataloging, and preparation of materials for use will be done in a central place for a number of schools, using all kinds of machinery and equipment for the speeding up of the finished product. Such a processing center will produce cards for the central card catalog located in each school, and in addition will publish periodically multiple copies of book catalogs with frequent supplements. A master book catalog for all of the schools served by the processing center will be published annually, and will be used by each school to borrow materials from others in the system. Hopefully the local schools will have new and better techniques and machines for the entire area of circulation, as has already been done by many college and public libraries. Various duplicating and copying machines for use by library staff, faculty and students will be a part of library equipment. Electronic devices will be in common use. Transistaphones for the use of individuals as used at the Kresge Library in Oakland University, Rochester, Michigan, may be installed in high school libraries.[11] They can be useful in assisting with instruction in library techniques and tools. Students pick up a receiving head set at the circulation desk. As they follow definite instructional procedures, they actually perform a problem or exercise. At the circulation desk, a student assistant operates the central control unit of records and tapes.

School librarians need to watch for information put out by the

Library of Congress Automation Techniques Exchange (LOCATE), which has been established for the purpose of collecting and disseminating information about automation programs for libraries.

Location

Whether or not the library in the local school will be in a central location only or have additional branches depends on the size of the school, its architecture, patterns of organization, and the size of the staff. As library services expand, it may be best simply to increase the size of the central library. Otherwise, it will be necessary to expand in one of the following ways: (1) through branches in strategic areas, largely duplicating the most popular materials of the main library, (2) through separate subject-centered branches, (3) through separate branches containing materials of one type or format; for example, one could contain films and filmstrips; another recordings, transparencies, and kits; another books, magazines, newspapers, and pamphlets. The following advantages and disadvantages of auxiliary centers must be carefully studied before a decision is reached:

Advantages

1. Quick and easy access to materials from the teaching areas and study centers is possible.

2. The professional librarian responsible for the auxiliary resource center serves a smaller number of teachers and students, and has the opportunity to know them and their needs better.

3. The professional librarian may more easily visit classrooms and become identified with the faculty of the subject or grade level that is his special responsibility.

4. It is sometimes more feasible to add auxiliary resource centers than to expand existing library facilities.

5. Auxiliary resource centers may become independent study centers or the major part of such centers.

6. The provision of additional spaces throughout the school encourages independent study and use of materials.

7. Professional librarians can be assigned according

to their competency in specific subjects or special areas of work.

8. Auxiliary resource centers provide the flexibility of access needed to meet the demands of team teaching, ungraded groups, and large schools' enrollments and physical facilities.

Disadvantages

1. Increased budget for duplication of materials is necessary since most materials in the auxiliary resource centers should also be provided in the central library, and possibly in more than one auxiliary resource center.

2. Additional professional and clerical library personnel will be needed to staff each center.

3. Problems in cataloging materials exist, since the user should be helped to find which materials are in the auxiliary resource center, which are in other resource centers, and which are in the central library only. Each auxiliary resource center must have a catalog, and the central library's catalog must indicate locations of all materials.

4. Dispersal of materials tends to fragment knowledge and to limit the user of an auxiliary resource center in his search for information.

5. Breadth of opportunity for browsing may be curtailed for the user who visits only one resource center.[12]

Regional Centers

Another possibility for the future as schools demand broader library service is the extensive development of regional service in a single school district, as is seen in a few places today. Located in the town of Salem, Utah, the Nebo School District has such a center. This Center serves as a supplement to the materials in the library of each school in the district. As of January, 1967, the Center contained about 3,000 filmstrips, 340 films, 3000 transparencies, and a number of tape recordings and multi-media kits. Teachers and other school personnel have access to the contents of the Center through a book catalog and its supplements. By simply telephoning to the Center, a teacher can find out immediately if a certain item is available for the time when he wants it. The Center's booking clerk records what item is wanted, and the delivery clerk who works on a regular schedule takes it to the teacher's school for his use. Any item can be kept for as long or short a time as the teacher requests it, and it is picked up on one of the regular trips made to each school by the delivery clerk. Other services which the Salem Center offers are: printing, photography, making transparencies. Among plans for future service is the production of video tape.

Organized in a different way are the regional materials centers of Pennsylvania.[13] Fourteen of the twenty-five centers now in existence are composed of multi-county groups; others are single county operations, single school districts, or multi-district organizations. In 1966, these centers had around 10,000 filmstrips, over 500 records, 300 sets of slides, 200 tape recordings, 250 museum kits, 600 art reproductions and some transparencies, dioramas, and models. In addition to circulating these materials, the centers have an in-service training session for their use for all teachers.

Personnel

Future needs in the area of library personnel will call for employees with a wide variety of abilities and educational preparation for positions at state, regional, and local levels. They will fall into three categories: clerical or secretarial, technical, professional. There will continue to be many tasks best performed by clerks especially trained to work with library materials and routines. Technicians may very well be working with electronic devices not yet produced, and their abilities to work with the technical aspects of a variety of audiovisual media will be necessary for the smooth operation of the library. Professional personnel will include people with competence in the administration and use of all kinds of media as well as subject specialists. The title, "media generalist," as proposed by James W. Brown of San Jose, California, State College may be used in place of "librarian." This title has the advantage of implying knowledge of both printed and audiovisual materials.

Education for School Librarianship

The entire program of education for school librarianship will need to be carefully scrutinized, both as it relates to education for other kinds of librarianship and also in light of the modern concept of the school library having a great variety of materials and many new services. As more and more books and other materials are obtained by the local school already processed, the emphasis in the library science curriculum for school librarians will move away from the technical processes in the direction of required courses in guidance in the use of materials. Student-librarianship or work experience will be an accepted part of all curricula for school librarianship. The requirement that school librarians must also be certified as teachers will probably continue. Whether school librarians are chiefly librarians or chiefly teachers is obvious in the attitude toward their education. With the present move toward required degrees beyond the bachelor's for teachers, the position of the American Library Association and other leaders that acceptable library science education requires a fifth year degree will be strengthened. Thus the courses required for teacher certification are taken at the undergraduate level. Some people advocate that the master's degree be in education and the library science courses be in the undergraduate program. The important background of general knowledge needed by the school librarian as well as the requirements of courses in education and librarianship must not be neglected.

Little progress will be made in supplying professional personnel for existing vacancies as well as the many new positions if the critical shortage of library school faculty which now exists is not alleviated. The controversy concerning the requirement of a doctor's degree as a requisite for teaching at the college and post-bachelor's level exists in the field of library science as well as in others. Some leaders of the profession think of it as the primary criterion for selection of library school faculty, while others believe that it should be of secondary importance. "...the profession can no longer afford this status-seeking on the part of the schools. The 'first criterion' for a teacher should be teaching ability, and the second, perhaps, is relevant background and experience. The Ph. D. might be desirable but it certainly should not be paramount."[14]

The activities and publications of the Library Education Division of the American Library Association and also the Association of American Library Schools indicate that these groups are studying the problems of curriculum and education for various kinds of librarianship. Two conferences held at the University of Illinois in 1967--one for teaching faculty and administrative officers of library science programs concerning the need for effective evaluation of student performance, and the other an international conference on the whole realm of education for librarianship--also demonstrate real concern in this area.

There is room on the school library staff for teachers with strong subject backgrounds of both undergraduate and graduate work and with minimum hours in library science. However, the head librarian (or media generalist) should have at least a master's degree in library seience. An interesting picture of the school library staff of the future was presented by Beauell M. Santa as far back as 1960.[15] Mrs. Santa saw the librarian as being a member of a group of closely coordinated specialists working in the total school program. Experimentation and creativity would characterize his activities which would be more like those of a teacher than a technician.

As a result of different organizational patterns, expanding curricula, more study in depth, a great variety of learning materials, and new technology, studies of the needs for various kinds of library personnel will be made. It is hoped that these studies will result in a clearer picture of their duties than now exists, as well as a recognition that newly created positions will be a necessary part of the library staff.

Research

Research studies of all aspects of the school library are greatly needed. For example, the Jennings-Lubrizal Program for School Libraries, an experimental study now going on at Western Reserve University, will have results of interest to all school librarians. As individual schools and school systems experiment with new programs, the facts must be written down and made available.

Thus, as school libraries have evidence that they are necessary for quality education, the needed understanding and financial support will be forthcoming. Assistance from the Office for Research and Development of the American Library Association can be expected by school librarians, as well as from other organizations.

The future will see requests for more and broader school library service. Hopefully, state, regional and national groups will lead the way in revising existing standards to meet these demands. At the national level, the American Association of School Librarians and the Department of Audiovisual Instruction of the National Education are working together on Standards for Educational Media Programs.

The librarian who administers today's school library has a large responsibility. His belief that all kinds of learning materials are best administered and utilized through the library is of paramount importance as he makes plans for the present and the future library needs of the local school. He must be knowledgeable in the selection of a variety of materials and their organization; and above all, expert administration calls for giving the best possible service and maximum use of the library.

With the attractiveness of many of the audiovisual materials and the tremendous advertising that goes on for them, the librarian is tempted to buy these materials simply because they are new and are different from books. In the big task of selection, he must always keep in mind the needs of his school and what kind of material is best suited to each need.

Good organization of materials is a major responsibility of the library administrator. Here he needs to keep in mind the objective of easy access to the contents of the library. The administration of the library quarters is no simple task. The librarian has to figure out where new materials are to be processed, old ones mended, supplies and equipment stored, good working areas for the production of materials, seating areas, traffic patterns, and to provide viewing and listening facilities. In addition, circulation and reference functions must be organized, and personnel's duties decided on.

It is easy to get "bogged down" in these administrative responsibilities and to think that one has a successful library when all of these aspects are operating smoothly. Regardless of how many carefully selected materials the library has, how well organized they are, and how large and well trained a staff is available, the extent and nature of the library's services is the only reason for its existence. As the best ways of serving students in each school situation are discovered, new and challenging directions can be expected for the school library.

Notes

1. Education USA, February, 1966, p. 102.

2. See Appendix VI for list of current federal legislation affecting school libraries.

3. NICEM: Index to 16mm Educational Motion Pictures, Mc Graw-Hill Book Co., 330 W. 42nd St., New York, N.Y. 10036

4. Automated Cataloging News, March, 1967, University of Southern California, School of Performing Arts, Division of Cinema, University Park, Los Angeles, California 90007

5. University Microfilms, 300 N. Zeeb Rd., Ann Arbor, Michigan. 48106

6. 3M Company, 2501 Hudson Rd., St. Paul, Minnesota 55119

7. Max U. Bildersee, "Beginning the End of Tape Library Chaos," Educational Screen and Audiovisual Guide, XLVI (January, 1967), 43.

8. Television Information Office, 745 Fifth Ave., New York, N.Y. 10022

9. Communication Films, 870 Monterey Pass Rd., Monterey Park, California 97154

10. Joseph L. Wheeler and Herbert Goldhor, Practical Administration of Public Libraries, Harper and Row, 1962, p. 18.

11. Floyd M. Cammack, "Radio Active Library," Library Journal XC (October 15, 1965), 4300-4302.

12. The Knapp School Libraries Project... op. cit.

13. Marcus Konick and Benjamin Jenkins, "The Regional Instructional Materials Center in Pennsylvania," Audiovisual Instruction, XI (September, 1966), 554-557.

14. "Too Late for the Doctor," [editorial] Library Journal, XCI (October 15, 1966), 4908.

15. Beauell M. Santa, "A Librarian's Responsibility..." In Images of the Future; A Report of the Institute held at the Univ. of San Francisco, April 30, 1960. The School Library Assn. of Calif. (Northern Section) and the Calif. Assn. of Secondary School Administrators.

Selected Readings

General Considerations

Atlick, Richard D. "Education, the Common Reader, and the Future," ALA Bulletin, LX (March, 1966), 275-282.

Boula, James A. "Development of Instructional Materials Centers in Illinois," Illinois Libraries, XLVIII (February, 1966), 118-124.

Brown, James W. "AV Library: Complement or Merge?" Educational Screen and Audiovisual Guide, XLVI (January, 1967), 22-23+

Havighurst, Robert J. "Educational Changes: Their Implications for the Library," ALA Bulletin, LXI (May, 1967), 537-543.

"Innovation in Education," Educational Technology, Spring, 1967. (series of articles)

Shera, Jesse H. "What is Past is Prologue; Beyond 1984," ALA Bulletin, LXI (January, 1967), 35-47.

Federal Aid

Burke, Arvid J. "U. S. Control of Schools 'Will Grow'," American School Board Journal, CLIII (November, 1966), 26-27.

"Federal Aid to Education," Education, LXXXVI (May, 1966), 515-545.

Includes articles giving excerpts from the Guidelines and Standards for administering Title II in Colorado, Ohio, and Oregon. Also includes Information Chart: Federal Aid to Education 1966.

Mahar, Mary Helen. "Federal Legislation and Programs to Assist School Libraries," ALA Bulletin, LX (February, 1966), 153-156.

National Education Association. Dept. of Rural Education. PACE: A Guide for Developing Projects to Advance Creativity in Education. Washington, D. C., 1966.

Overlan, S. Francis. "Federal Grants: Can You Get One?" American School Board Journal, CLIV (April, 1967), 7-9.

Roney, Ruth Anne. The Doubleday Guide to Federal Programs: 1966-67; Elementary and Secondary School Libraries. Garden City, N. Y.: Doubleday, 1966.

"A Schoolman's Guide to Federal Aid - Pt. IV," School Management, X (December, 1966), 60-91.

A detailed report of federal aid as it affects schools.

Materials

Archer, N. Sidney and Samuel M. Sanzotta. "Administrative and Instructional Adjustments Resulting from the Use of Programmed Materials," Audiovisual Instruction, IX (November, 1964), 608-609+

Forsdale, Louis and others. "A Point of View," Drexel Library Quarterly, II (April, 1966), 155-166.

Describes how 8mm film is practical for use in education.

Gilkey, Richard. "Instructional Media for Social Studies: A Glimpse into the Future," Educational Screen and Audiovisual Guide, XLV (November, 1966), 26-27.

Herbst, Harvey R. "KLRN's Second Year: a Bright Picture," Audiovisual Instruction, IX (November, 1964), 599-601.

Results of educational TV in Central Texas.

Limbacher, James L. "The 8mm Revolution," Library Journal, XCI (December 15, 1966), 6162-6163.

Names and addresses of 8mm producers are included.

Oestreich, Arthur H. "ETV and You," Educational Screen and Audiovisual Guide, XLVI (April, 1967), 26-27.

"Paperback Boon Seen for Future School Libraries," Library Journal, XCI (September 15, 1966), 4238-4239.

Roper, Burns W. Emerging Profiles of Television and Other Mass Media: Public Attitudes, 1959-1967... Television Information Office, 1967. (pamphlet)

Shera, Jesse H., "The Librarian as Anthologist," Wilson Library Bulletin, LXXXIX (September, 1966), 89+

Witty, Paul A. "The Electronic Pied Piper - Enemy or Ally of Reading," Education, LXXXVII (September, 1966), 42-47.

Results of an annual study made during a 15-year period of the interests of Chicago children in TV and other media.

Quarters and Equipment

Licklider, J. C. R. Libraries of the Future. M. I. T. Press, 1965.

"Results of a 2-year inquiry into the applicability of some of the newer techniques for handling information to what goes at present by the name of library work."

Mary Alma, Sister. "Automated Instructional Materials Centers? The Future is Now," American School Board Journal, CLIII (December, 1966), 19-22+

Schwilk, Gene L. "Million Dollar Carrels," Library Journal, XCII (January 15, 1967), 306-308.

Spring, Bernard P. "'Plug-In' School: Next Step in Educational Design," Architectural Forum, CXIX (August, 1963), 68-73.

Toffler, Alvin. "Libraries," In Bricks and Mortarboards. [New York] Educational Facilities Laboratories, Inc., [1964] pp. 71-98.

Although describing college libraries, this section has many interesting ideas for physical plants and new materials worth considering for school libraries.

Personnel

Carnovsky, Leon. "Changing Patterns in Librarianship: Implications for Library Education," Wilson Library Bulletin, XLI (January, 1967), 484-491.

Miller, Robert H. "The Media Specialists: Broward County, Florida," Audiovisual Instruction, XII (February, 1967), 132-137.

"Professional Librarians in Public Schools of Wisconsin," In Professional Librarians: An Inventory of Personnel and Personnel Needs in Wisconsin... Madison; The Library School, University of Wisconsin, 1965. pp. 8-10. (mimeographed)

Shane, Harold G. "Current Issues Facing Leadership in the School Library Field," ALA Bulletin, LX (October, 1966), 923-926.

Appendix I

Excerpts from The Students' Right to Read

The National Council of Teachers of English, 1962, pp. 8-9

The right of any individual to read is basic to democratic society. This right is based on the only tenable assumption for democratic living: that the educated free man possesses the powers of discrimination and is to be entrusted with the determination of his own actions.

The right to read, like all rights embedded in our constitutional traditions, can be used wisely or foolishly. In many ways education is an effort to improve the quality of the choices which are the exercise of this right. But to deny the opportunity of choice in the fear that it may be unwisely used is to destroy the freedom itself. For this reason, we respect the right of individuals and groups to express their views for the guidance of others. But for the same reason, we oppose efforts by individuals or groups to limit the freedom of choice of others or to impose their own standards or tastes upon a community at large.

In selecting books for reading by young people, teachers of English consider the contribution which each work may make to the education of the reader, its aesthetic value, its appropriatness to the curriculum, and its readability both in structure and content for a particular group of students. Many works of literature important in our culture contain isolated elements to which some individuals may object. The literary artist is a seeker after truth, recording in structured form life as he perceives and feels it. As a creator, he must necessarily challenge at times the common beliefs or values of the culture, for creation is the process of identifying new relationships out of which come new meanings. In seeking honestly for meanings behind reality, the artist strives to achieve a work of art which is always basically moral, although not necessarily conventionally moral. Moreover, the value and impact of any literary work must be examined as a whole and not in part--the impact of the entire work transcending words, phrases, or incidents out of which it is made.

The teacher must exercise care to select works for class reading and group discussion which do not place students in a position of embarrassment in open discussion with their peers, but he must also be free to recommend for individual reading any work he feels will have educational significance for an individual student. In addition the teacher needs the freedom to discuss with a student any work that the student reads whether the teacher has recommended it or the student has discovered it for himself...

Appendix II

Selection Tools for the Secondary School Library

Tools for Selecting all Kinds of Material

Free and Inexpensive Learning Materials. George Peabody College for Teachers, 21st Ave. South, Nashville, Tennessee 37205 Frequently revised.

Selected Free Materials for Classroom Teachers. Fearon Publishers, 2165 Park Blvd., Palo Alto, California 94306 Gives over 500 sources of free print and non-print material available in 1965.

Selecting Materials for Children and Young Adults. Children's Services Division and Young Adult Services Division, ALA, 1967.

The Teacher's Guide to Media and Methods (Formerly School Paperback Journal) 124 East 40th St., New York, N.Y. 10016 Monthly September through May. Articles as well as reviews of selected new paperbacks, films and other materials.

We Read; Selected Lists of Children's Books and Recordings. Children's Services Division, American Library Association, 1966. Free from Office of Economic Opportunity, Community Action Program, Washington, D. C. 20506 Lists books and recordings for preschool children through age 16 "that may be particularly helpful in work with disadvantaged children and especially applicable in Community Action projects."

Tools for Selecting Books: General Lists

"Adult Books of 1966 Significant for Young People," Top of the News, XXIII (April, 1967), 293-294. Annually selected by the Young Adults Committee of the Young Adult Services Division of ALA. Brief annotations.

A Basic Book Collection for High Schools... 7th ed. American Library Association, 1963. Includes annotated list of periodicals considered as first choice recommendations.

A Basic Book Collection for Junior High Schools... 3rd ed. American Library Association, 1960. Includes list of magazines.

...Best Books for Children...1966 edition... R. R. Bowker Co., 1180 Ave. of the Americas, New York, N.Y. 10036
Annotated selection of 3700 books in print, for grades K through 12. Annual compilation.

Book Reviews. Young Adults Cooperative Book Review Group of Massachusetts. Appears periodically. Available on subscription basis from Mrs. Leila-Jane Roberts, Winchester Public Library, Winchester, Mass. 01890

The Booklist and Subscription Books Bulletin. American Library Association. Published semi-monthly except monthly in August. Includes detailed evaluation of new reference books. Quarterly reviews of films. Reviews of audiovisual materials may be expanded.

Books for the Teen Age. New York Public Library. 1301 Ave. of the Americas, New York, N. Y. 10019 Annual compilation.

Catalog of Paperbacks for grades 7 to 12. 1963. The Scarecrow Press, Inc., 257 Park Ave. South, New York, N. Y. 10010

Choice. American Library Association. Monthly. New books evaluated by teachers of undergraduate courses in liberal arts colleges and by librarian subject specialists.

Doors to More Mature Reading: Detailed Notes on Adult Books for Use with Young People. Young Adult Services Division, ALA, 1964.

The High School Librarians Choose the Best Books of '66 for their Readers. Bureau of Library Services, Baltimore City Public Schools, Oliver and Eden Streets, Baltimore, Maryland 21213

Junior High School Library Catalog... 1965. The H. W. Wilson Co., 950 University Ave., Bronx, N. Y. 10452 With 4 annual supplements.

The Paperback Goes to School, 1967/1968; a Selected List of Elementary and Secondary School Titles. Selected by a Committee of members of the NEA, the AASL and the NCTE.

Popular Paperbacks for Young Adults. 1966. Young Adult Services Division, ALA. "Titles and topics popular with young adults in projects, training schools, Jobs Corps, and public library programs."

School Library Journal. 9 monthly issues. R. R. Bowker Co., 1180 Ave. of the Americas, New York, N. Y. 10036
As well as brief reviews of new books, there are frequently special lists of paperbacks, professional reading,

free and inexpensive pamphlets. Interesting and timely articles are included. SLJ Reviews on Cards also available from Bowker on a subscription basis.

Standard Catalog for High School Libraries... 8th ed. 1962. With 5 annual supplements. The H. W. Wilson Co., 950 University Ave., Bronx, N. Y. 10452

Tools for Selecting Books to Meet Special Needs

The AAAS Science Book List for Young Adults, compiled by Hilary J. Deason. 1964. American Association for the Advancement of Science, 1515 Massachusetts Ave., N.W., Washington, D.C. 20036

About 100 Books... A Gateway to Better Intergroup Understanding; compiled by Ann G. Wolfe. 5th ed. 1965. Institute of Human Relations, 165 E. 56th St., New York, N.Y. 10022
Selected for readers preschool through 16 years of age.

Books for Brotherhood. Annual compilation. National Conference of Christians and Jews, 203 N. Wabash Ave., Chicago, Illinois. 60601

Books for the Job Corps. 1965. R. R. Bowker Co., 1180 Ave. of the Americas, New York, N. Y. 10036
A guide to leisure reading for Job Corps trainees. Prepared by the Boston Public Library Staff as a book-buying list for the Job Corps camps.

Books in American History; a Basic Book List for High Schools, by John E. Wiltz. 1964. Indiana University Press, Bloomington, Indiana. 47401

"Easy Books for Slow Senior High School Readers," by Milbrey L. Jones. Top of the News, XXI (April, 1965), 205-209.

Educator's Guide to Free Science Materials, compiled and edited by Patricia H. Suttles. 6th ed. 1966. Educator's Progress Service, Randolph, Wisconsin. 53956

Gateways to Readable Books; an Annotated Graded List of Books in many fields for Adolescents who Find Reading Difficult, by Ruth Strang and others. 4th ed. 1966. The H. W. Wilson Co., 950 University Ave., Bronx, N. Y. 10452

Good Reading for Poor Readers, compiled by George Spache. rev ed. 1962. Garrard Publishing Co., 1607 N. Market St., Champaign, Illinois. 61821

"History Paperbacks for the High School," by G. J. Rausch. Reading in High School, I (Summer, 1964), 103-105.

Human Relations: A Basic Booklist, produced by an education committee of the Madison (Wis.) Public Schools. 1966. Order from Curriculum Dept., Madison Public Schools, 545 W. Dayton St., Madison, Wisconsin. 53703
Elementary through senior high school. Includes fiction and non-fiction.

"Learning to Listen: Books on Music for Young Adults," Top of the News, XXIII (November, 1966), 72-76.

Outstanding Biographies for College-bound Students. 1965. Young Adult Services Division, ALA.

Outstanding Fiction for College-bound Students. 1965. Young Adult Services Division, ALA.

Outstanding Theater for the College-bound. 1966. Young Adult Services Division, ALA.

"Paperback Miracle; an Inexpensive Library for Music Teachers and Students," by G. J. Buelow. American Music Teacher, XIII (January, 1964), 9+

Reading Ladders for Human Relations, edited by Muriel Crosby. 4th ed. rev. 1963. American Council on Education, 1785 Massachusetts Ave., N.W., Washington, D.C. 20036
Arranged around six human relations themes, lists books for primary through the adult reader.

Suggested List of Books Useful in the Program of Instruction for the Non-English Reader. 1963. Bureau of Libraries, Board of Education, New York, N. Y.

The Teachers' Library: How to Organize it and What to Include. 1966. National Education Association, 1201 16th St., N.W., Washington, D.C. 20036

Vocations in Biography and Fiction... compiled by Kathryn A. Haebich. 1962. American Library Association.

World Affairs Guides, by Leonard S. Kenworthy. Includes: Selected Resources for Studying the World, Studying Africa, Studying South America, Studying the Middle East. 1962- Bureau of Publications, Teachers College, Columbia University, 2960 Broadway, New York, N. Y. 10027

World History Book List for High Schools: Selection for Supplementary Reading. 1962. National Council for the Social Studies, 1201 16th St., Washington, D. C. 20036

World Understanding: a Selected Bibliography, compiled and edited by Alice H. Flynn. 1965. Oceana Publications, Inc., Dobbs Ferry, New York. 10522

Published for the United Nations Association of the United States of America, Inc. Extensive annotated lists of selected books and pamphlets, with a brief listing of visual aids, exhibits, flags, maps, and posters.

Tools for Selecting Reference Books

"Current Reference Books;" a monthly review of selected titles, by Frances Neel Cheney. Included in each issue of *Wilson Library Bulletin.*

General Encyclopedias in Print; a Comparative Analysis. 1967. R. R. Bowker Co., 1180 Ave. of the Americas, New York, N. Y. Revised annually.

Guide to Reference Books, by Constance M. Winchell. 8th ed. 1967. American Library Association.

Reference Books; a Brief Guide for Students and other Users of the Library, compiled by Mary N. Barton... 6th ed. 1966. Enoch Pratt Free Library, 400 Cathedral St., Baltimore, Maryland 21201

Reference Materials for School Libraries: Grades 1 through 12. 2nd ed. 1966. Publication No. 385. North Carolina Department of Public Instruction, Raleigh, North Carolina 27601

Subscription Books Bulletin Reviews, 1964-1966. American Library Association

Tools for Selecting Magazines

Dobler World Directory of Youth Periodicals, by Lavinia G. Dobler. 1966. Schulte Publishing Co., 80 Fourth Ave., New York, N.Y. 10003

101 Plus Magazines for Schools Grades 1-12, compiled by Ruby Ethel Cundiff. 1964. Tennessee Book Co., Nashville, Tenn. 37205

Periodicals Related to International Understanding. Educational Materials Laboratory Report, April 2, 1963. Educational Materials Laboratory, U. S. Office of Education, Washington, D. C. 20202

Tools for Selecting Pamphlets

"Annual Review of Curriculum Materials," edited by Dorothy M. Fraser. *Social Education*, XXIX (April, 1965), 228-237+ Lists curriculum guides available for purchase or free distribution from various school systems.

Anti-Defamation League of B'nai B'rith Publications. 315 Lexington Ave., New York, N.Y. 10016
Publishes pamphlets and a few books on Totalitarianism and Extremism, Civil Rights, Prejudice, Anti-Semitism, Race Relations, and related subjects. This organization also has a human relations audiovisual library containing materials which can be purchased or rented.

Selected Science Services. U.S. Office of Education.
Numerous lists of pamphlets and occasionally books, magazines, and audiovisual materials. Not limited to Government publications. U.S. Supt. of Documents, Government Printing Office, Washington, D.C. 20402

Selected U.S. Government Publications. Weekly publication. U.S. Supt. of Documents, Government Printing Office, Washington, D.C. 20402

Vertical File Index. Monthly publication. The H. W. Wilson Co., 950 University Ave., Bronx, N. Y. 10452
Selected pamphlets and some books, from many sources.

Tools for Selecting Audiovisual Material: General Lists

Audiovisual Instruction. 10 monthly issues. Dept. of Audiovisual Instruction, National Education Association, 1201 16th St., N.W., Washington, D.C. 20036
Although primarily containing articles in the field, each issue includes "Index of Audiovisual Reviews."

Educational Screen and Audiovisual Guide. Published monthly. 434 S. Wabash, Chicago, Illinois 60605
Although primarily containing articles in the field, each issue contains "Film Evaluations," "Filmstrips," "Audio." Each August issue contains the "Blue Book of Audiovisual Materials." The August, 1966, issue contains "over 1000 listings of materials released since August, 1965."

Guides to Newer Educational Media, by Margaret I. Rufsvold and Carolyn Guss. 2d ed., 1967. American Library Association.
Describes catalogs, services, professional organizations, and periodicals which regularly contain information on new media.

Non-Book Materials for Have-Not Youth... Prepared for use at The Young Adult Services Division Preconference, Two Blocks Apart, July 8-10, 1966... Young Adult Services Division, American Library Association.
Includes: statement on using films and other non-print materials with "have-not" youth; names and addresses of film distributors, companies providing exhibits; annotated,

selected lists of films, recordings, and art prints.

Tools for Selecting Films and Filmstrips

A Directory of 16mm Sound Feature Films Available for Rental in the United States. 1st edition. 1966. Published by Continental 16, Inc. Distributed by Educational Film Library Association, 250 W. 57th St., New York, N. Y. 10019

EFLA Evaluations. Card service. Educational Film Library Association.

Educators Guide to Free Films. 26th ed. 1966. Educators Progress Service, Randolph, Wisconsin. 53956
Annual publication. Not selective.

Educators Guide to Free Filmstrips. Educators Progress Service, Randolph, Wisconsin. Annual publication. Not selective.

Films for Children; a Selected List. 1966. Children's and Young Adult Services Section, New York Library Association.

Films for Libraries. 1962. American Library Association.

Films for Young Adults; a Selected List. 1966. Children's and Young Adult Services Section, New York Library Association.

Landers Film Reviews, edited by Bertha Landers. 10 monthly issues. Landers Associates, 4930 Coliseum St., Los Angeles, California. 90016 Annotations on loose-leaf sheets.

Library of Congress Catalog: Motion Pictures and Filmstrips. Library of Congress, Washington, D. C. 20540
Quarterly publication. Not selective.

Tools for Selecting Tape and Disk Recordings

An Annotated List of Recordings in the Language Arts for Elementary Schools, Secondary Schools, Colleges, edited by Morris Schreiber. 1964. National Council of Teachers of English, 508 S. Sixth St., Champaign, Illinois. 61820

Audio Cardalog, edited by Max U. Bildersee. Card service. 10 monthly sets. The Cardalog, Box 989, Larchmont, New York. 10538

Library of Congress Catalog: Music and Phonorecords. Library of Congress, Washington, D. C.
Semi-annual publication. Not selective.

National Tape Recording Catalog, 1962-63. Also Supplement 1, 1965. Department of Audiovisual Instruction, National Education Association, 1201 16th St., Washington, D. C. 20036

Tools for the Selection of Pictures, Kits, Programmed Instruction, and Television Program Materials

Art Reproductions, by Jane Clapp. 1961. The Scarecrow Press, Inc., 257 Park Ave., South, New York, N. Y. 10010

Lists reproductions in the fields of painting, graphic arts, sculpture, and decorative arts, available from U. S. and Canadian museums.

Asia Kit. The Asia Society, 112 E. 64th St., New York, N.Y. 10021 Includes: (1) various pamphlets, (2) A Guide to Films, Filmstrips, Maps and Globes, Records on Asia, (3) Asia: A Guide to Basic Books, (4) Asia: A Guide to Children's Books, (5) A Guide to Paperbacks on Asia, (6) Asia: A Guide to Traveling Exhibitions and Displays.

Color Slide Survey Sets of Architecture, Sculpture, Painting, and the Minor Arts from Paleolithic Times to the Present... 1965. American Library Color Slide Co., Inc., 305 E. 45th St., New York, N. Y. 10017

Instructional Television Materials: A Guide to Films, Kinescopes and Videotapes available for Televised Use. 3rd ed. 1964. National Instructional Television Library, 10 Columbus Circle, New York, N. Y. 10019

Learning from Pictures, by Catherine M. Williams. 1963. Department of Audiovisual Instruction, NEA, 1201 16th St., N. W., Washington, D. C. 20036

Programs, '63: A Guide to Programmed Instructional Materials. U. S. Office of Education. No. OE-43015-63 U. S. Government Printing Office, Washington, D. C. 20402

Teachers Manual for the Study of Art History and Related Courses... Color slide catalog. 1964. American Library Color Slide Co., Inc., 305 E. 45th St., New York, N. Y. 10017
Lengthy list of individual slides and sets in a wide range of art history fields. As well as serving as a selection aid, this volume is a valuable reference tool as it gives an outline of art history.

Appendix III

How Libraries and Schools Can Resist Censorship

Statement Adopted February 1, 1962
by the American Library Association Council

As a normal operating procedure, every library, and the administration responsible for it, should establish certain principles.

1. There should be a definite book selection policy. This should be in written form and approved by the board of trustees, the school board, or other administrative authority. It should be stated clearly and should be understood by members of the staff. This policy should apply to other materials equally, i.e., films, records, magazines, and pamphlets.

2. A file recording the basis for decision should be kept for titles likely to be questioned or apt to be considered controversial.

3. There should be a clearly defined method for handling complaints. Any complaint should be required to be in writing, and the complainant should be identified properly before the complaint is considered. Action should be deferred until full consideration by appropriate administrative authority.

4. There should be continuing efforts to establish lines of communication to assure mutual understanding with civic, religious, educational, and political bodies.

5. Newspapers of the community should be informed of policies governing book selection and use. Purposes and services of the library should be interpreted through a continuing public relations program, as should the use of books in the school.

6. Participation in local civic organizations and in community affairs is desirable. The library and the school are key centers of the community; the librarian and school administrator should be known publicly as community leaders.

If an attack does come, remember the following:

1. Remain calm. Don't confuse noise with substance. Most attacks come from small groups of people who have little community backing. Time after time the American people have shown that, given the facts, they will back solidly the responsible exercise of professional freedom by teachers and librarians and that they will insist on protecting their own freedom to read. Insist on the deliberate handling

of the complaint under previously established rules. Treat complainants with dignity, courtesy, and good humor.

2. Take immediate steps to assure that the full facts surrounding a complaint are known to the administration. The school librarian should go through the principal to the superintendent and the school board; the public librarian, to the board of trustees or to the appropriate community administration official; the college or university librarian, to the president and through him to the board of trustees. Full, written information should be presented, giving the nature of the problem or complaint and identifying the source.

3. Seek the support of the local press immediately. The freedom to read and the freedom of the press go hand in hand.

4. Inform local civic organizations of the facts and enlist their support where possible.

5. Defend the principles of the freedom to read and the professional responsibility of teachers and librarians rather than the individual book. The laws governing obscenity, subversive material, and other questionable matter are subject to interpretation by the courts. The responsibility for removal of any book from public access should rest with this established process. The responsibility for the use of books in the schools must rest with those responsible for the educational objectives being served.

6. The ALA Intellectual Freedom Committee and other appropriate national and state committees concerned with intellectual freedom should be informed of the nature of the problem. Even though each effort at censorship must be met at the local level, there is often value in the support and assistance of agencies outside the area which have no personal involvement. They often can cite parallel cases and suggest methods of meeting an attack. Similar aid in cases affecting the use of books in the schools can be obtained from the Commission on Professional Rights and Responsibilities of the National Education Association.

Appendix IV

"A Summary of the Major Quantitative Standards for School Library Programs"

Standards for School Library Programs

by The American Association of School Librarians, Chicago: American Library Association, 1960, pp. 24-25

Note: This summary table is to be used after the complete text of the book has been read. These quantitative standards must be interpreted in relation to a complete and active school library program.

Type of collection	Delegated administrative responsibility	Location in the school
The Collections of Printed Materials		
The collection in the school library	Head School Librarian	1 School library area or areas, with seating space for at least 45-55 in schools with 200-550 students or fewer and for 10% of the student enrollment in schools having 551 or more students. 2 Classroom collections on short- or long-term loans from the school library.
The collection of professional materials for the school faculty	Head School Librarian	A separate room, either as part of the school library suite or in another part of the school.
The collection of supplementary materials. (Sets of supplementary texts; classroom reference materials)	Head School Librarian	1 May be housed in a separate area, in the textbook room, or in storage-stack space of the school library. 2 Classroom collections on short- or long-term loans.

The Collection of Audio-Visual Materials

	Head School Librarian or Co-ordinator of Audio-visual Materials, depending on local school policy and organization	1 The audio-visual center (may be part of the school library suite or a separate center near the library). 2 Classroom collections in short- or long-term loans.

Annual expenditures	Size of the collections	Personnel
The Collections of Printed Materials		
1 Funds for regular library books: in schools having 200-249 students... at lease $1,000-$1,500. In schools having 250 or more students... at least $4.00-$6.00 per student. 2 Additional funds as required for: Encyclopedias, unabridged dictionaries, magazines, newspapers, pamphlets. Rebinding. Supplies and equipment.	1 Books: Minimum size of the collections in schools having 200-999 students... 6,000-10,000 books. 1,000 or more students... 10 books per student. 2 Magazines: a At least the following number of titles in the general magazine collection in schools having Grades K-6 25 Grades K-8 50 Jr. high schools 70 Sr. high schools 120 b Plus at least 5 titles in the areas of librarianship and instructional materials. 3 At least 3-6 newspapers. 4 An extensive collection of pamphlets covering a wide range of subjects.	1 Librarians: For the first 900 students or fraction thereof: 1 librarian for each 300 students or major fraction thereof. For each additional 400 students or major fraction thereof: 1 librarian. 2 Clerks: 1 clerk for each 600 students or major fraction thereof.
1 For materials, a minimum of $200-$800, depending on the needs and size of the faculty and the availability of other collections of professional materials in the community.	1 Books: At least 200-1,000 titles, the number depending on the needs and size of the faculty and the availability of other collections of professional materials in the community.	

2. Funds for supplies and equipment.	2 At least 25-50 professional magazine titles. 3 Other instructional materials as needed.	

The Collection of Audio-Visual Materials

1 Not less than 1% of the total per pupil instructional cost ($2. 00-$6. 00) for the acquisition of audio-visual materials. 2 Funds for supplies and equipment.	1 A sufficient number of types of audio-visual materials for use in the classrooms, in the school library, and for home use. 2 Films used 6 or more times a year are purchased. 3 Filmstrips and recordings used more than once a year are purchased.	1 When the head school librarian has partial administrative responsibility for audio-visual materials, the number of librarians and the number of clerks is each increased by 25%. 2 When the head school librarian has full administrative responsibility for audio-visual materials, the number of librarians and the number of clerks is each increased by 50%.

Appendix V

Professional Organizations

1. American Library Association, 50 East Huron St., Chicago, Illinois 60611

   Membership includes a subscription to the _ALA Bulletin._ Annual dues are based on salary.

   Membership entitles you to enrollment in one Type-of-Library and one Type-of-Activity Division free. Divisions recommended for school librarians:

   Type-of-Library Division: American Association of School Librarians. Includes subscription to _School Libraries._

   Type-of-Activity Division: Young Adult Services Division. Includes subscription to _Top of the News._

2. National Education Association of the United States, 1201 16th St., N. W., Washington, D. C. 20036

   Membership includes a subscription to the _NEA Journal_. Annual dues: $10

3. Department of Audiovisual Instruction of the National Education Association, 1201 16th St., N. W., Washington, D. C. 20036

   Membership includes a subscription to _Audiovisual Instruction._ Annual dues: $10

Appendix VI

Federal Legislation Affecting School Libraries

Elementary and Secondary Education Act of 1965. Public Law 89-10

Title I. Financial assistance to local educational agencies for the education of children of low income families. Salaries of staff, construction of facilities, library materials and equipment can be obtained.

Title II. School library resources. To support provision of school library books, textbooks and other instructional materials.

Title III. Supplementary educational services and centers. Often referred to as PACE (Projects to Advance Creativity in Education). Materials and equipment for a materials center is a possibility here. Coordination with other Federal programs is encouraged, particularly with ESEA, Title IV. Projects involving non-public schools are encouraged.

Title IV. Educational research and training.

Title V. Strengthening state education agencies. Improve leadership resources of state education agencies. State school library supervisory services are available here.

National Defense Education Act of 1958. Public Law 88-665

Title III. Strengthening of instruction. To provide printed and audiovisual materials, other than textbooks, in the major areas of the curriculum; also for audiovisual equipment.

Title V. Concerns programs for guidance and counseling. Printed and audiovisual materials in guidance may be included.

Title VII. Experimentation and development of new educational media.

Title XI. Training and supervision of personnel. Supports institutes for advanced study for teachers and supervisors in specific subject fields, for educational media specialists, and for librarians.

Economic Opportunity Act of 1964. Public Law 88-452

Title I, Part B. To provide training and work experiences for unemployed young people through participation in state and local work-study, work-training, and Job Corps programs. This is an opportunity for school libraries to obtain additional clerical help.

<u>Title II, Part A.</u> Urban and rural community action programs in poverty areas. School librarians can give assistance by conducting story hours or having the library open in the evenings as a place to study.

<u>Higher Education Act of 1965.</u>

<u>Title II.</u> Scholarships and fellowships for experienced teachers in the major curricular fields, and for specialized personnel including librarians.

<u>Vocational Education Act of 1963.</u> Public Law 88-210

Directed toward strengthening vocational and training programs in specialized high schools or in high schools having a vocational education department. Funds for librarians' salaries and for library materials may be obtained when they are directly a part of the vocational program.

<u>National Foundation on the Arts and Humanities Act of 1965.</u>

For the acquisition of equipment related to the arts and humanities, for centers similar to those provided under ESEA, Title III; for training institutes to strengthen teaching in these areas.

Index

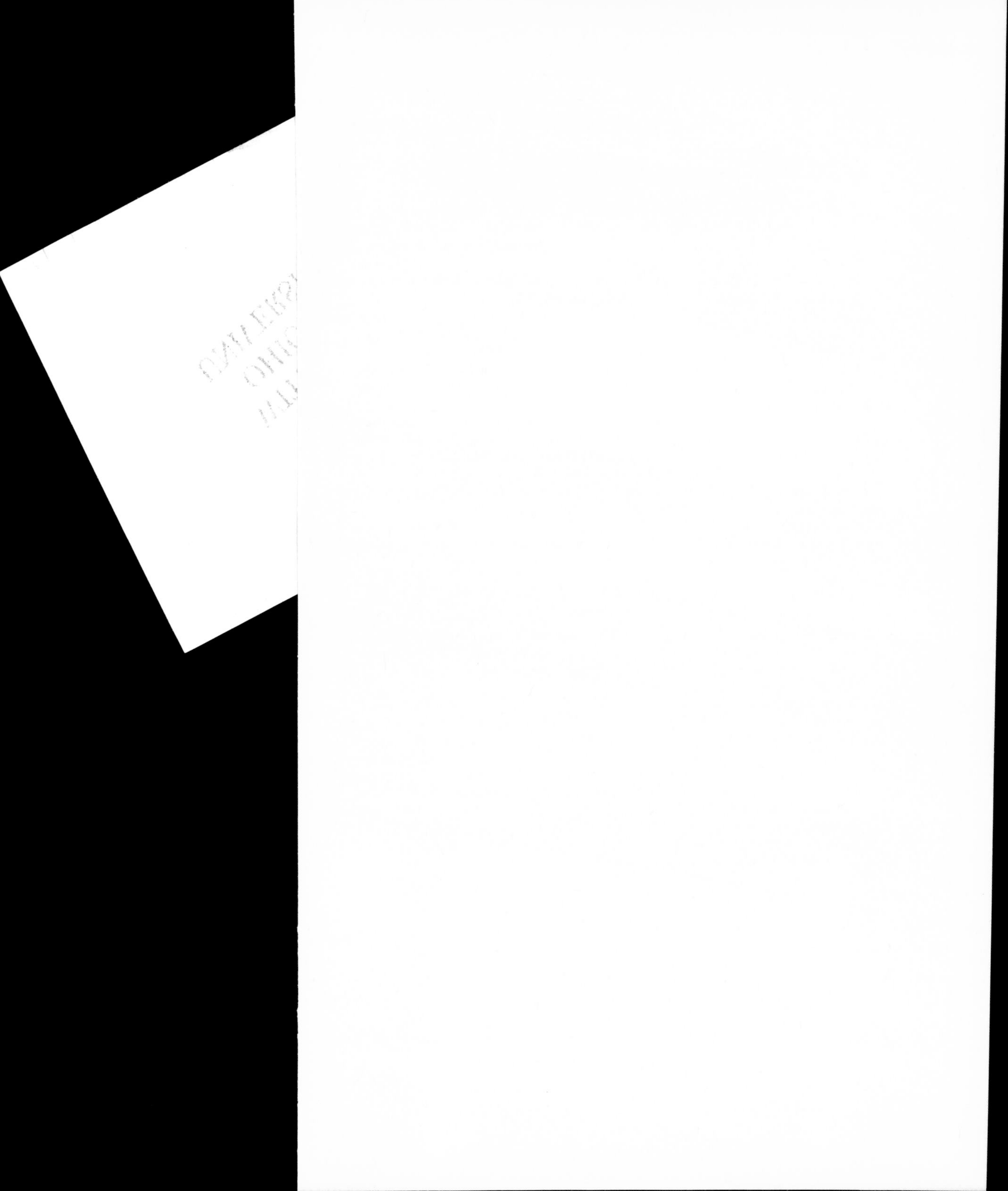

WITHDRAWN FROM
OHIO NORTHERN
UNIVERSITY LIBRARY
RETURNED
DEC - 5 1972
PRINTED IN U.S.A.
GAYLORD